# Writings of George Godwin

## Stewart Jackson, MD

Order this book online at www.trafford.com
or email orders@trafford.com

Most Trafford titles are also available at major online book retailers.

1. Homesteader – Great War veteran--Writer—
Lawyer--Romantic

Stewart Jackson, MD
North Vancouver, BC
sandjjackson@shaw.ca

Writings of George Godwin
Stewart Jackson, MD

Jacket photograph George Godwin, Great War veteran
Courtesy of Godwin Books, Victoria, BC
Jacket design by Maru Photography
maruphoto@shaw.ca

Printed in the United States of America.

ISBN: 978-1-4269-4990-6 (sc)

*Trafford rev. 01/24/2011*

**Trafford**
PUBLISHING®   www.trafford.com

**North America & international**
toll-free: 1 888 232 4444 (USA & Canada)
phone: 250 383 6864 ♦ fax: 812 355 4082

# Acknowledgements

I am grateful to Shawn Lamb, Collections Manager/Archivist in Nelson, British Columbia; Fiona Colbert, Biographical Assistant, Johnian Office, St John's College, Cambridge and Miss J.E. Small, Headmaster's PA, St. Lawrence College, Ramsgate, Kent. Robert Thomson of Godwin Books in Victoria, British Columbia provided valuable advice and a copy of Godwin's journal. Lucy Godwin, George's granddaughter, who fondly remembered her grandfather, gave insight and information about the family. Fred Braches whose critique of "The Eternal Forest" was so helpful and who led me to Lucy.

# Contents

# Introduction

George Stanley Godwin was an intense romantic, whose writings told of a varied and sometimes troubled life, though with an understanding of the world about him far ahead of his time. Godwin wrote twenty-one books, two of which were brought back into print in the 1990s, left behind parts of a journal and correspondence to a young love. A prodigious writer, many of his books are written in the third person and are in part autobiographical, or contain his very personal views, which, along with his journal and correspondence, allow the story of his life to be constructed.

As a teenager he hated school and was banished from home in England to Dresden with his sister. With his new wife he crossed the world to homestead in the "eternal forest" of the Fraser River valley in British Columbia but failed miserably. He experienced the mud and rats and psychological terror of the trenches of the Great War. Invalided out of the war to a distant sanatorium where, away from home and family, he fell in love with an occupational therapist, a love hidden for half a century. He wrote about the Temple in London and his efforts as a lawyer and twenty-one books on varied subjects. He bore the emptiness of the death of a son.

The tale begins with his earliest memories.

# Childhood

George Godwin was born in London on the first day of July in 1889, the second youngest of eight children in a typical middle class Victorian family. With three sisters to spoil him, his first years were those of sisterly care and brotherly disinterest. His mother already had six older children to concern and worry her and his father, who was a successful wholesale meat marketer, had more on his plate than young George. George didn't really remember his father who died when he was three. He had only two distinct recollections of his father. On one occasion, bursting open the door of the dining room to find his mother and father sitting talking, he received a sound whipping for breaking in on them. At that time George had but one sentiment towards his father, that of fear. He thought his father a hard man then but later, in the light of experience, he thought more kindly of him. What could a little child have known of the jaded nerves and irritability of an overwrought man suffering from cancer?

Was it his sisters' maternal behaviour or that of his mother that were his first memories? The fondest of those early memories were of his mother and how he would scurry across the landing from the night nursery to his mother's room in bare feet to be in bed beside her with the demand: "Mummy, tell me a tale!" Those tales were always touching and moral. Love always triumphed. He recorded that tears would rise in his eyes, a lump come in his throat. And his mother, Welsh with Huguenot blood in her veins, would be as affected by the pathos of the stories as much as he himself. Often they would cry together but he was never happier than during that morning hour with his mother. *

From his mother he learnt in simple language the stories of The Bible and The Lord's Prayer, which he did not understand. Jack the Giant Killer, Red Riding Hood and Hansel and Gretel were certainly more vital things to him than the Deity he was taught to pray to, but he reverenced what he did not comprehend because his mother reverenced such things. He wrote.

*Hardly should a little child feel with an understanding heart for the Man of Sorrows. The story lies dormant throughout the immature years, but in later life, when sorrow is a reality and suffering a part of life, the tragic tale of old shines out from the mind with a new and poignant meaning.*

By his father's death his mother was left with the responsibility of looking after a family of eight. On his eldest brother Bert fell the task of replacing the head of the family and whilst yet in his teens Bert became a man of affairs. He took what fate gave him with a quiet patience and for many years was accepted as the breadwinner as a matter of course.

---

* Much of the details of George's childhood, holiday and school experiences are taken from his journal jottings. To be faithful to those writings his language and words take precedence in this account.

George's Father died in their London house, while the children were away at Port Reculver on the Kent coast, where the family had a country house. They spent the summers in Kent and the rest of the year in London.

George described the London home as one of those substantial old houses that stood back from the road. Behind the house a garden that ended with stables and glass houses, the stables having access to a back street. There was Gyp the bull terrier, always on the leash, being considered too ferocious to be allowed his freedom – a reputation earned through killing, in honest chase, an inconsequential kitten. George had no fear of Gyp, knowing his reputation ill deserved. Many were the Sunday afternoons spent beside his kennel regaling him with as much of the morning's sermon that George could comprehend. But Gyp was not all. There were his rabbits, white mice and chickens.

Such was his garden and such were the inhabitants if he omitted his brother with whom he played. But he was not so easily dealt with as Watts, the coachman or Gyp or the rabbits. George's brother Dick was 18 months older, fair and sturdy and lacking a complete set of front teeth. He had fallen from the esplanade at Port Reculver and struck his mouth on a breakwater. To Dick George was always "Slippy", his faithful servitor, his abject admirer. Dick was George's first hero if not, alas, his last. Willful, wild Dick! He was never really tamed; instinctively he turned toward the open places of the world. Streets and offices were not for such as he. Men like him belonged in the times of Elizabethan England.

His vices were pronounced. He lied shamefully and taught George the art. He led George into bad company with street boys and schooled him in fighting with them by thrashing him quite frequently. He did things that in later years George may have despised him for but he never lost affection for him because he possessed the one quality that compensates for many weaknesses: he was always generous, amazingly openhanded and beneath his turbulent nature there beat the heart of a woman.

Port Reculver lay on the north coast of Kent near Herne Bay within easy reach of the train line from London to Ramsgate. Reculver is at the site of the roman town Regulbium, the birthplace of Christianity in England where Augustine had landed in 597AD. To the west of the town shelved the sloping cliffs that had been converted into miniature Alps by the aggressive waves and winds of the North Sea. As George spanned the seas from the cliff tops his youthful imagination may well have led him to dream of the eleventh century Earl Godwin, Earl of Wessex, the most powerful Earl in the Kingdom. Who knew, perhaps an ancient ancestor? Godwin was advisor to the Danish King Canute and helped fight his battles. How many fallen warriors now lay under the waters that covered ancient land off the coast of Wessex? Godwin's first wife was Canute's sister and Harold, the eldest son of his second marriage, later succeeded Edward the Confessor as King of England.

This ancient soil became the children's chosen hunting ground and it was there that brothers Dick and George would spend long summer days. In their code scorn of fear was the principal tenet. To admit the hazard would have been unforgivable and, if in the secret heart of either of them fear lurked, the more would its existence be given the lie by foolhardiness. Together they climbed and scrambled. Now it would be Dick who, lying full length, would lower George to some cranny in search of gulls' eggs. Oh, the wild heart beatings on those occasions! Below, the surf breaking in a long white line upon the shingle, and sending up its rhythmic music. The face of the cliff glistening in the sun, the nest all but within reach, the voice above counseling: "Steady, Slippy! How many of them are there? Can you reach?" And then what heart beats! The slow, slow stretching out, the balance regained, the throat of Slippy beating as with Thor's hammer providing protection from impending doom. Then the pull up to safety again, generally with the spoil a yellow sticky mess in the pocket. How the gulls wheeled and cried maledictions on the despoilers! What did they care for the heart of a mother-gull? An egg? They had no hearts then.

At the west end of the seafront lived Captain Rogers, the brothers' staunch friend and ally in wrongdoing. The retired skipper of some windjammer, the old man conducted a 'Bathing Establishment', an occupation that allowed him to watch through his telescope the passing ships bound for the four corners of the earth. He was a figure who stood for the romance of strange places. The boys were lured by his tales of the unknown. In Dick and George he engendered a wanderlust that led George to bush life on the Pacific Coast and Dick to the wild places of Africa where the skins of lions and the tusks of elephants took the place of the crushed yellow sporting trophies of earlier days.

In the Captain's dinghy they would push off from the beach at dusk. In their imaginations sailing a pirate junk. Dick was the Pirate Captain and Slippy the bloodthirsty crew. Out to where the white yachts were riding at anchor they would pull. Silently drawing alongside the faithful Slippy would clamber up the bowsprit and creep down the deck to peer in at some party of card-playing yachtsmen. Sometimes a quick retreat down the bowsprit stays would be the result of discovery, then away from the Revenue Cutter to some other strange craft riding peacefully at anchor where the sinking sun shed long streamers of golden ribbon along the water.

They were never caught at pirating but had they been, George knew that it would have been just so much evidence of the necessity for them going to school. What did elders know of Truth and Romance? To the boys, the boarding of a merchantman, armed to the teeth, was an exciting and commendable business. But boys keep these things to themselves unless there be an understanding heart like the heart of old Captain Rogers. The sisters regarded such exploits as outrages, just as they did when the rabbits were painted green, but neither of those worthies had the imaginations of artistic temperaments.

One day, having had some minor sickness, George was permitted to go for a walk on the esplanade. George recalled the events that followed in his journal.

*Once there I sat down to read a Robin Hood story. Presently there came along a tall person wheeling a cycle. He sat down beside me. Now, although I loathed going to church on Sunday and generally was sore put to it to get through the service, I had a childlike reverence for this surpliced priest. He was not, I thought, as other men.*

*This tall man spoke to me and enquired of a good hotel where lunch might be had – he knew far better than I – but that was not a matter for a small boy to see through. I told him of an hotel, a big one on the Parade. Then he flattered me by telling me of a recent visit he made to the Holy Land. The Holy Land forsooth... With the insidious cunning of a Jesuit he suggested that I ask permission to go out with him that afternoon. He would have a bicycle for me; I could say that he was a clergyman my father knew; I knew him, did I not? If permission were granted it was arranged that I should go to the hotel after lunch and he would hire a bicycle and we would ride out to the old Castle some 4 miles away. He would like to see it.*

*We rode out to the old castle, the priest and the boy. At the 'Castle Inn' we left our machines and walked along the high cliff. There the man of God did that which set me running to the Inn, terrified. He caught me up, that wily priest, and with soft words silenced me and back at Glenrock sealed my silence with as much sweetmeats as I could carry.*

*And so while I was child I became contaminated by one who, by profession, followed the lowly Nazarene. I wonder: do such men ponder the saying of Master Christ that it would be better for him to cast himself into the sea with a millstone about his neck?*

When the fate that hovered over the two brothers in those heady days finally descended they were packed off to a small preparatory school at Glenrock in Sussex. George must have been eight or nine. He had not been there long when he received a letter one day from his mother telling him of Captain Roger's death. George was isolated with measles and alone at the time. Looking out over the housetops to whence the sea was whipped white by the March wind, he thought for the first time of death. It meant that old Captain Rogers would never look through that telescope again or pinch his leg and ask had he good knickers on. He cried, that was his first sorrow.

It was the next summer at Reculver that Dick first developed a liking for the town boys. One evening George and he quarreled. What it was about was forgotten– they quarreled so often but always made up directly they got their wind again. It was in the evening. Dick together with a number of tradesmen's messenger boys was playing some game on the way home. The result of the quarrel George never forgot.

*We fought. There before those boys he beat me (not that I didn't put up a good fight) but he beat me as he generally did. Filled with shame and rage (shame that I should have been beaten by my brother before those townsboys and rage that my brother should have done it) I ran home as fast as ever my feet would carry me. There was one fixed resolve in my mind: I would kill my brother. Arriving at the gate I crept silently in and through the garden to the woodshed. Taking a long and heavy piece of wood I crept back and took up my position behind the gate pillar. There I waited, choked with*

15

*sobs of rage and with hate gnawing at my heart. It became dark. He was afraid to come home, I felt sure of it, but I waited on. He would come through the gate and then I would hit my hardest.*

As he looked back on that evening that he so nearly became a Cain George was convinced that thoughts of consequences never entered his head. That the law possibly would have considered him *doli incapax*, so young as to be incapable of deliberate criminal malice, too young to distinguish clearly between right and wrong, he neither knew nor cared. His moral training was obliterated by the primal passion that convulsed him. His brother came in that night through the stables so that in his conscience remained only the knowledge that once in his life he lived through the mental phase of murder. So before he was near his teens *"I knew something of the emotions, having experienced virulent hate with a desire to kill, overwhelming sorrow, and then and until the end a profound love for my Mother."*

At the age of fourteen George was sent to Saint Lawrence's School in Ramsgate a mile or two in from the coast. He was to leave the sheltered preparatory school to follow Dick, who had already been there for a year, and his friend, Jack Drake. The preparatory school had been conducted on the lines of a home and the Principal, who boasted no degree or other pedagogic qualification, made up for this shortcoming with a large-hearted nature. George was sorry to leave the school with its homelike life but he hankered to follow Dick and his friend.

In leaving home for Ramsgate George probably took the same route as the family every summer to their summer home at Reculver on the London, Chatham, and Dover Rail line. It was a familiar route as the tracks followed the south side of the Thames River through Greenwich, Dartford and Gravesend. On reaching Faversham the train veered North towards the sea where at Whitstable George's heart would have turned to memories of summer careless pleasures and happiness. But this was different, a new and less inviting prospect waited beyond Herne Bay and Margate. After a couple of hours of apprehension the train carrying George would have puffed and rocked its way into the Harbour Station at Ramsgate.

St Lawrence's School lay inland a mile or two. George may have walked up the High Street and Margate Road and turned right onto College Road to the imposing buildings that had been the former home of South Eastern College before it became the School and later the College of St Lawrence, or taken a horse and carriage, his mind clouded by what was to come. The grounds of the school were extensive with distant views of the Kent seaside. His mother would have shown him an advertisement she had received extolling: "A Church of England Public School, the constitution of which provides that the religious teaching shall be in accordance with the principles of the Reformation." In accord with these principles George learned in the first few days at the start of the Michaelmas term in 1903 that every pupil was expected to read his Bible morning and evening and to kneel by his bedside for a few moments before beginning his day's work and retiring to rest.

He soon found that his brother and his friend had formed new associations and the first day at school marked the opening of the gulf between his brother and himself. What they had in common as small boys, they had in common with all small boys: fishing, swimming, smoking cigarettes. But now he was faced with what may be called a clique. However much Dick might have wanted him to be one of them, the others were of a different way of thinking, which was as well, as it turned out. Dick's friends enjoyed a certain notoriety as a gang of boys whose chief amusement was the organized tyranny of those weaker than themselves. New boys were their favourite game. Dick's predisposition towards the townsboys of Reculver manifested itself again when he selected the hectoring, ragging element at school; as his associates. So it came about that the brothers drifted apart.

The first few days were miserable enough and George often wished himself back at the little school where the scholars sat at one large table with the Principal and his wife. His chum Jack had found new friends too and this defection hurt more than that of his brother.

So it was that George faced the miniature world that a public school is, alone. His advantages were few, his drawbacks many. Among so many he was shy, almost afraid. He lost confidence and often had difficulty when answering a master to refrain from tears. Possibly he was suffering acutely from that malady, homesickness. And homesickness like seasickness too often is regarded as the subject of jests. George wrote about those first trying weeks at his new school.

*In any case, my sensations were mostly of a disagreeable nature. I longed for privacy, and there was none. The end of the day was to me one round of tortures, discomforts and embarrassments. I realized vividly enough that the only way in which I could hope for peace would be to tackle my most aggressive tormentor and beat him but how was this to be done? The tormentors took care always to select those smaller than themselves. Nothing can be easier than to strike the weak, to follow with the mob, to point the finger of derision at the splendid few who scorn the wisdom of their generation. Men do these things and boys do them too. The boy is the father of the man and a school is the world in miniature.*

*I was the only new boy in that dormitory and I had to furnish the evening's entertainment. This varied from evening to evening. Sometimes I would be bundled into the clothesbasket and once the lid was on the game appeared, so far as one could judge from the somewhat confined quarters, to consist of well-sustained efforts to break every bone in my body. Towel-flipping, superfluous cold douches and the sousing of my bedclothes varied the programme. That I was eventually left unmolested I can only attribute to the fact that it was discovered that I could tell stories of Robin Hood and his merry men and variations on the romances of Jules Verne.*

*The hours of school were so many hours of blank inertia. I was too unhappy to pay much attention. I had no desire to learn the subjects that were taught, or rather, to learn them as they were taught. I therefore closed my mind to the voice of the master and in a world of dreams awaited the ringing of the bell. I surreptitiously consumed many books, mostly exciting stories of adventure. I seldom lost my place at the bottom of the class, except in English, History and Scripture when I contested the other end. And as the Saint Lawrence system prescribed corporal punishment for mental ineptitude – even when it often enough was the ineptitude of the master – I regularly came in for a caning on Fridays.*

*Such was the price I paid for the consolation of private readings.*

*So much did I hate the imprisonment of that great red-brick pile, with its walls and its ordered playing fields, the soulless routine of the white-washed classrooms, the hairy hands of the form-master who prosecuted me, that I determined to run away to sea. I had saved pocket money for two months and had written to every aunt and uncle I possessed, asking for money. I packed the things I meant to take and had fixed the hour for the great escape: the half holiday, when, not being down to play for the second eleven of my House, I intended to ask for leave to pass beyond bounds – and bolt!*

*But why didn't I bolt? It was a moral inhibition, a certain spiritual fastidiousness. I turned back and faced the balance of the term simply because I had envisaged too vividly the feelings of my mother when she should hear of my total disappearance. I had wept silently as I pictured her anxiety and distress. And so the next day, just to show the folly of my quixotry, I got into trouble, yet again, and received a thrashing at the hands of the school sergeant. The headmaster, being a clerk in Holy Orders, was too fastidious to handle the switch in person!*

George found solace in the evening chapel service. He sang in the choir and found consolation in the music. The words of the Te Deum conveyed some vague promise to him of a future compensation for present ills. The poetry of the psalms stole over him and he found a sensuous enjoyment in the volume of the organ music. He was not religious but those services were to him at that time what the music of Wagner came to be some years later. He felt they took him to the verge of the unknown, quickened in him hitherto unknown emotions, and intensified a longing, hardly recognized, to love something. In those moments of emotion he ached to pour out a love – how, or upon whom, he knew not, but this knowledge would come later.

In just a year, at the age of fifteen, he was to leave the place where he had failed to impress and was thoroughly unhappy.

# Dresden

In a family council it was decided that George should go to Germany with his sister Maud who was to continue singing training in Dresden. In a year or two he would need to come to some conclusion about his future career. He had to do something someday and at sixteen that day was getting nearer. A brisk breeze was blowing down the Channel when George, his mother and sisters went out with the steam packet from Dover. As they stepped aboard George looked up to where the Castle stood on the high cliffs and remembered the days when he fought mock battles over the down.

Dresden, a city of music. There George learned German and became an admirer of the works of Wagner, Schumann and Goethe. He was introduced to Siegfried, to Parsifal, Lohengrin, the Legend of the Holy Grail and the mythology that Wagner utilized so wondrously. In his dreams he saw Lohengrin, son of Parsifal, Knight of the Holy Grail, standing in a shell boat drawn by a swan, coming to Elsa's cause round the bend in the blue waters of the Zwingerteich, his armour glowing brightly, a silver swan mounting his helmet and blazoned on his shield.

Those were happy days. He had no work to speak of and was free to amuse himself. The country ablaze with colour was a joy always. The wide shiny streets so clean, so prosperous looking.

Living in Dresden, Schumann-Heink made her first of many phonograph recordings in 1900. She was well known for her performances of

Wagner works at Bayreuth. Emil Berliner, the inventor of the flat disc for recording, with his brother Joseph founded Deutsche Grammophon in 1898 in Hanover. The company immediately began to mass-produce shellac records on which could be heard the widely loved music of Wagner.

The sensuous enjoyment George had felt in the school chapel led him in Dresden as often as he could to cross the Neumarkt to the Frauenkirche. There to hear the wonderful silvery sound of the magnificent Silbermann organ that Bach had once played. George remembered magic nights of intoxication in the great theatre beside the slow wide Elba; there by the royal palace where ancient princesses of the royal line passed in and out in prim sedans, ignoring the passage of the centuries, clinging stubbornly to the romantic past. The first night of the *Ring* and everywhere the hum of voices. The utter silence as the conductor raised his wand and the first sweet notes floated up to the gallery, up to rapt students, each one marking the music from an open score.

Dresden in the spring, with its broad clean streets garlanded with blossoming trees, pink and white. Loafing through the Saxon Switzerland to Königstein. Long days tramping, singing in the sun. Beer gardens and fat waiters, dark, cool drafts of lager. To the Weisser Hirsch, up the hill crowned with white cherry blossom, and, amid the trees, the little tables, each with its family group, each with its long thick beer steins. Every Saturday, every Sunday.

And everywhere friendly faces, the broad, homely Saxon faces of the people in the streets, of the boys in the *Realschule.* They had no playing fields, those German schoolboys, knew nothing of cricket on warm summer afternoons, or football in the tang of autumn air. For them sedate walks, two by two, in the Grosser Garten. Haunted boys, pursued by the spectre of the cursed *Einjähriger.* This was the One Year Examination, which if failed, meant one must serve a full three years as a private soldier. If one passed, then only one year and with concessions. Those that failed told tales, unpleasant tales. Tales of brothers who had failed and who as conscripts, had been spat upon, who had been clouted with a sheathed sword, had had toes stamped upon.

A woman known as Red Rosa had written a book, *Rosa Luxemburg Speaks*, exposing these things and was cast into prison for it. It was dangerous to have the book in one's possession. Rosa a co-founder of the German communist party who "advocated socialism with a human face" was later shot and killed by soldiers.

The concessions for those who passed were many. Boys could meet as friends. George recalls Zeidlitz for example.

*That wide smile, those friendly blue eyes. His greatest ambition was to learn das englische boxen. And Stolze, grave and preoccupied, anxious always for the examination, but absorbed in his hobbies, inviting you to share his pleasures, inviting you to accept his friendship, in the classroom, in his home, in his little sanctum. There he painted, proudly showing a canvas. The Erl King upon his steed, riding through night and storm, clasping his child. And that was not all, the fiddle*

24

*tucked under his chin from which yellow hair sprouted amid the pimples, he would play Schumann's Ich Grolle Nicht and Schubert's Du Bist die Ruh.*

For George Christmas evoked memories of gay lighted trees in every home with their red, white and blue sparkling balls and twinkling candles. *Heilige Nacht,* the old hymns. And Frau Schmidt, stout kindly soul, insisting that George take the sofa, place of honour, since he was an *Auslander* and far from home. A foreigner! As if one could be anywhere more at home than in Germany, ever among kindlier, dearer friends. A decade later these were the boys, now men and soldiers that he would be pitted against in the trenches of France. How could one square that war with such memories of Dresden, so many kindnesses, so many friends, so many happy days? Imagine it: sticking a bayonet into friendly grinning Zeidlitz; imagine bombing romantic Stolze! *

And yet he pondered the mood of other men. The swaggering officers of the Wilhelmstrasse, Wiesbaden and how they pushed civilians aside, both men and girls, like so much dirt. And the incident in the Dresden shop when two American ladies were arrested for commenting disrespectfully about the portrait of the Kaiser.

---

*These thoughts must have been penned many years later after the war and his time in the trenches of Vimy Ridge.

25

But then, in the middle of the first decade of the new century, his time in beautiful, cultured Dresden came to an end. Returning to England his newly acquired command of the German language found George occupation in London in a German bank. The years went by, the routine of a city clerk's drab life, as with the regularity of an automaton. He hated the life, worked, paralysed by some dimly comprehended inhibition. Fear perhaps. He witnessed: *"the long, overcrowded train draw up at the dingy terminus, and the debouchment of those swarming units that went to the making of the world's financial heart. Little, self-important molecules bent upon reproduction in unending cycles of time, working for the next generation, preoccupied, blind."*

To try to relieve the frustration of his life as a bank clerk and the daily drudgery of travel from Crouch End to the city centre he started to read and study Law. With some pride on May 26, 1909, he was admitted to the Society as a Middle Templer. George was later called to the bar in absentia on November 17, 1917. Did the members know that he had been sent home on sick leave from France and was now part of the Reserve Battalion, or did they think he was at Passchendaele at the end of the third and final battle of Ypres? Whatever it was, he was not notified and only learnt of their acceptance of him sometime later.

# The Eternal Forest

Why was it that, at the age of twenty-two, George and his young bride, the daughter of a Belfast physician, traveled half-way around the world to British Columbia and the Pacific coast? Was it his despair at toiling in a bank, or the lack of prospects after a year or two in lowly chambers of the Middle Temple, or the recent loss of his mother, or the urge to travel planted in him by his brothers? Dick, for example, had left for Samoa to oversee a copra plantation. More likely it was his profound disenchantment with the pettiness and snobbery that were often rife in the genteel English social class from which he came.

George wrote about the couples' time in British Columbia some years later in a book titled *The Eternal Forest Under Western Skies.* The book was published in 1929 and reissued in a slightly edited version under the title *The Eternal Forest* in the mid 1990s. His journal notes written in 1913 and 1914 contained information that was included in the book during it's writing in the 1920s.

The book is almost certainly somewhat autobiographical, but uses as the main character someone called "newcomer" rather than the first person. The names of the various characters he and his wife meet and their behaviors are mainly fictitious but their experiences very much fit what would have been expected of the times. Fred Braches, a respected local British Columbian historian, in a detailed analysis of the book, (especially exploring linkage of the characters described by Godwin with actual persons of the

27

time), begins to separate fiction from some verified facts of the Godwins' short time in Whonnock, on the banks of the Fraser River. *

When the book was first published in 1929 it caused a great deal of unrest in Whonnock. It was relatively easy for people to recognize themselves and others despite the name changes created by Godwin. His descriptions of the people were felt by some to be in error, unkind and disrespectful. He even attributed a murder quite wrongly and the book was ignored or rejected by the local people. The book was indeed a novel and therefore could be allowed to embellish reality. In his reading of the book and writing of the Godwins' time in Whonnock this author has tried to concentrate on recorded data and the most likely facts. As well additional confirmation of dates and descriptions of characters in the book are taken from notes made in his journal from December, 1911 until November, 1914. Included, however, are Godwin's descriptions of the trials and tribulations that most surely faced many homesteaders in the Fraser Valley and the Vancouver region in the years before the Great War. Godwin's description of the tensions that existed between various ethnic and racial groups vividly highlights the early problems of the emerging Vancouver.

The book is an interesting read with colourful descriptions of the time, but has very clear deviations from historical reality. Braches has

---

* Braches, Fred. Ferguson's Landing: George Godwin's Whonnock. Whonnock Notes, 6. Whonnock, 2000.

pointed out many of the issues at question in relation to the characters he purports to have met.

Godwin's granddaughter has confirmed dates that can be verified and conflict with events described in the novel. Lucy Godwin (nee Riley) recalls that George's wife Dorothy came from a wealthy Victorian Belfast family well used to genteel society. To bring such a lady to the wilds of the Fraser Valley in late Edwardian times was surely unwise. The Godwin family was also quite well-to-do and although George claims to have had only 500 pounds on leaving England, it is probable that he or his wife had access to considerably more funds.

In the book Godwin tells how they came to Canada as a married couple though in truth he came first to prepare the way for his fiancé to join him later. He probably came in much the same way as he fantasized they might have come as a pair in his novel. The first annotation in his journal in December, 1911 was from Calgary where he may have rested for a time before proceeding to British Columbia.

For whatever reason, Dorothy and he, with *"five hundred pounds sterling"* in their pockets, sailed the North Atlantic to Montreal and took the Trans Continental Canadian Pacific train which George described as *"a world of gold, a world that rolled out under a cobalt sky – the fecund prairie ripe for harvesting. A climb up to the clouds from the Albertan foothills where, from the roof of the world pale mists streamed like banners from glittering peaks"*.

Beyond Banff they would have gazed through the plate-glass windows of the dining-car over a world that reached as far as the eye could see, "*into the violet haze of a far horizon. Range upon range, the mountains swept across the landscape. Like colossal monsters, crouched upon their bellies, they seemed, wallowing in the blue waters of the lakes, their blunt snouts burrowing down into the valleys, while upon their great flanks the timber bristled like some hairy growth*".

George would have found it wonderful and awe-inspiring to creep precariously over vast and dizzying trestle bridges, high above the tumult of swollen mountain torrents. Unforgettable to creep, clinging like some monstrous beetle, along the stark face of precipitous mountain sides; to descend steep grades and roar, with clanging bell, into the dark mouths of rock-hewn tunnels bored into the mountain's heart.

But it was at Whonnock, on the banks of the Fraser River in 1912 that they chose to leave the train. After all this spectacular beauty the green, timbered settlement revealed itself with a vague sense of disappointment. The valley slept, green and still, in the shadow of the bush.

Perhaps the first suggestion that the title of the book should include the word "eternal" came from a short piece Godwin wrote in September, 1912 about the Capilano Canyon in North Vancouver.

*Below the emerald waters of the canyon gleam,*
*Above the ramparts of the gorge up-rise,*

30

*Eternal glorious canyon set in green!*

*So limped pools of Paradise may seem,*
*Seen in celestial dream, with earthly eyes,*
*Where God and all his angels walk serene.*

As they climbed down from the tourist coach, *"a white-coated negro porter swung down with their leather portmanteaux and stood by expectancy written on his bland face. The station agent came forward and told them to come and see if all their "junk" was put off. He said it in a tone that implied that they had served him a bad turn. There was nobody to greet them."*

George names the person who later came to meet them as Bob England. In truth England would have greeted George alone when they first met. He describes England as someone who was never punctual and in time arrived at the depot as the tail-end of the transcontinental train disappeared in a whirlwind of dust and ashes through the rock-cut three miles below the settlement.

There must have been prior arrangements to leave the train at Whonnock rather than to go those further few miles to Vancouver. The man called Bob England was probably Robert Fletcher a person known to be living in Whonnock at the time. Fred Braches tells us that Fletcher was a long time resident of Whonnock who had migrated from England in 1886. He married the daughter of Ole Lee from Trondheim in Norway. Aside from farming and other things he could do to make money, Robert was active as a realtor for the area. Godwin may well have been attracted to British Columbia by one of Fletcher's advertisements published by

31

Rogers, Black and McAlpine in Vancouver for whom Fletcher acted as an agent. A typical advertisement promoted "Fertile Farm Lands, Whonnock" and promised "Fruit Farms, Chicken Ranches and Vegetable Gardens in five and ten acre blocks of first class land, needing very light clearing on a beautiful southern slope." The land that Fletcher sold to Godwin was five acres, put together from three and two acre portions of neighbouring properties immediately adjacent to a larger parcel owned by Fletcher himself. It is no great stretch for Godwin to have used Bob (Robert) England (Fletcher, an English immigrant) as a pseudonym for the man who Godwin claimed in the book sold them their land and met them from the train at Whonnock. The property is shown on a survey map of 1912 as "Godwin's Land" and remains intact to this day. It lies close to 269th Street and 98th Avenue in the present day District of Maple Ridge.

In the book George tells us that Bob was dressed in high boots caked in mud which had accumulated through three winters and was now coated with the dust of a dry summer. This suggests that Godwin arrived in Whonnock in the late summer of 1912. However, in May, 1912 Godwin wrote a "nocturne" from Coquitlam B.C.

*Silence, but not complete, for I hear the cry of a night-bird as it takes its way swiftly. Darkness, but not completely dark is the night, for a silver crescent shows itself above the shadowy forms of the trees. Sweetness, aye, sweetness, but for the bitter memory of nights since gone into the shadowy past, even as yon bird into the shadow of the wood.*

*In the Heavens myriad stars spangle the heavens shedding soft light aided by the new-born moon.*

*If we listen now, we hear the grass as it moves its numberless little blades, and grows, while the daisy, its tiny petals snugly closed sleeps until the kiss of the morning sun awakens it.*

*Everywhere Peace, and Sweetness, Nature is playing her Silent Nocturne of Peace, which only her Children may hear and hearing cherish as her greatest boon to them.*

Godwin describes Bob England's faded blue pants patched at the seat and his dinghy yellow canvas shirt lacking the lowest portions of the sleeves. He was smoking a corn-cob pipe and his hands were thrust deep into his pockets. He sauntered up, removed his pipe, raised his hat and asked. "*You got my letter I take it? My rig's outside, you must come up to the house first and feed and so on. Then I will take you round and show you a few places. Feel the heat? No? You will later. Valley heat is different from prairie heat, affects you differently. On the prairie the people boast of how much work they can get through in a day; here we brag about how little we can skin through with.*"

It was a novelty after the de luxe service of the express dining-car, to be eating a meal in a kitchen, and doubly a novelty to eat in a kitchen built of logs. Seated with Bob and his Norwegian wife [Georgina, daughter of Ole Lee Sr.] who quite casually told George that this was their first home. He was told that there were many places for sale but the prices were high because of a recent boom brought on by ill-founded optimism. These early years of the new century were later referred to as

33

heydays of optimism and unrestrained and uncontrolled capitalism. Bob England said it was a periodic madness. No good comparing conditions in the Old Country with here. For one thing, in British Columbia you must remember, every acre, every rood, had to be hacked out from the standing timber. It made a big difference. You could buy uncleared land for fifty dollars an acre, but it would cost two hundred to clear it.

The location they found George described as *"an enchanted location, looking down over the valley and the silver river to the far white mountains. Together, undisturbed, encircled by the bush."*

The toil of clearing the land began immediately. Though it may not have been as easy as the advertisements had suggested. Although George writes about clearing both alders and giant cedars the latter had in all likelihood been previously logged since this was second growth land. The book does not say where George lived in the first few weeks after arrival. Perhaps with Bob England and his wife. He was told that Old Anderson [another of the several Norwegian immigrants in the valley] would build the house. *"Old Anderson was slower than the second coming, but he was thorough. Just leave him alone. Thirty cents an hour, and he'll reckon up the odd minutes."*

Godwin's meeting with "The Norwegian" is recorded in his journal in July 1912 and his notes form the basis for the character Anderson. Plans had been drawn but Anderson ignored them. *"You want two bedrooms and a living-room, a kitchen*

*and, I think, an attic for young chicken and junk,"*
*he announced. "Here I will build it."* He pegged out
the site so that the kitchen door would be right
against a mighty fir stump and right upon the
northern boundary, as surveyed. George did not
want the house there. He wanted a garden, a small
garden which would shine all the more radiantly
because it would oppose its orderliness to the
clutter of the clearing, with its great uprooted
stumps, its tangle of vine-maples, its felled alders.*

George had no part in the building of the
house. Anderson built it and George carried and
fetched as bid, soon nailing on the soft cedar
shingles. A proud moment, making one's own
house! With Dorothy George hoped they would hug
to their hearts the illusion that this half-articulated
thing of yellow timber would take shape as the
house of their dreams. Some sort of miracle would
happen. This thing which had risen under the
hammer of the slow old man would change and
become their house, would stand complete and
perfect as they had devised it. A miracle, indeed!
When the yellow boards became walls and the roof
was in place, clothed in its red cedar, it was realized
with consternation that Anderson had made a
house in his own likeness: it was plain, rugged,
strong, very honest and very useful. The old man,
the book tells us, asserted his proprietorship by
praising it and then putting the seal of authorship

---

* The survey map of 1912 confirms that the
northern boundary of the property was indeed
immediately adjacent to the bush. The mighty fir
stump supports the previous logging of the area.

upon it by squirting a jet of tobacco juice on to the shrill new fir floorboards.

During the summer and fall of 1912 George visited New Westminster and Vancouver. His journal records his witnessing a group of native Indians gathered on a station platform at New Westminster in late August and in September a visit to the Capilano Canyon in North Vancouver.

The description of the house being built probably reflects reality although it was most likely built before George sent for Dorothy to come out to British Columbia to join him and become his wife.

The first mention of his wife in his journal is 'To Dorothy' written from Whonnock on January 15, 1913.

> *You came to me when I had squandered Youth;*
> *Strong your beauty and your Innocence;*
> *But strongest in your gorgeous gift of Love.*
> *You came, you loved and so you lifted me,*
> *A poor thing, stained and ignorant of Truth.*
> *You gave your love, that holy Frankincense,*
> *You wafted round me, so serene above*
> *All earthly things, I thought it was the key*
> *To heav'n itself, to come direct from God.*
> *. . . . . .*
> *And so you took me to you, loved me spite*
> *The Past that lingers yet, a smoldering fire.*
> *Did you dear heart, then pray a Lotus White*
> *Might spring to blossom from that early time?*

They furnished the house as best they could with oil paintings for the walls and a settee that came up the river by boat. They tried to keep up appearances by dressing for dinner, but this did not fit with their neighbours' ideas of life in the bush. They made attempts to maintain some semblance of upper class Edwardian manners. The enchantment of summer passed. Autumn murmured through the valley. It laid chill, invisible hands upon the bush. The forest trembled. The flaming maples stirred like giant torches, dripping gold and crimson fire, their dying leaves like great pools of blood, lay upon the ground.

A few months had passed when in February 1913 George allowed himself to pen some thoughts in his journal of "this simple life".

*There is not even a well. A little creek gives a supply of crystal water. After a week or two it becomes quite natural to draw the water from the creek as it is required and to carry it in buckets to the house. In the winter days the little trail down to the creek is muddy, but even the mud becomes familiar and inoffensive.*

*There is no coal or if there be any it is as yet unmined so that for us at least no man need spend his days in darkness hewing forests of other times. Our fuel is around us, and when we require warmth (which we always do during these winter days) the trees give it to us. Before a fire is possible some tree must be hewn down, sawn into lengths, split, and stacked by the fireside. And so as winter wears on there is a clearing in the bush and lamentations among the bleak, gaunt trees.*

The general store, which embraced the post office and performed the function of a bank, was about a mile distant down the hill and near the river. There the ranch produce (in the shape of eggs) could be traded for other necessities so that even money itself became, in great measure, indispensable. It was common practice to give credit in the store – a necessity in those cash-strapped times.

All day there was no sound but that of the countryside. George tells how the hens celebrated another egg with loud rejoicings, the rooster lifting up his voice melodiously. He goes on to report more of the sounds imagined or remembered. Out among the trees the resounding axe might echo merrily in the distance, punctuated by the groaning crash of some giant of the forest. The little woodpecker hammering on the bark of the birch until you wondered that the strenuous little fellow did not break his sturdy bill. With nervous little jerks, like some furry automoton, the chipmunk eyeing you from some mossy stump, and bolting at the first sign of animation in the stranger.

From the valley the shrill whistle of the locomotive was thrown about among the hills, the rumbling growing louder but never more than a metallic murmur then departs. But that did not concern the folk of the countryside. The train traveled by them, but its main business was with the city, where men lived close pent and walked upon hard stone and heard all day the multitudinous noises of the city.

To George each day yielded fresh delights. Although the book suggests that Dorothy also shared in those delights she surely found these a change, more a trial from the pampered life of the daughter of a wealthy family. Routine there was, the little creek to visit, the trees to fell, the flock to feed, and a multitude of other tasks, but each had its delight for George. The glorious swinging of the axe: Is that work? Well, the town dweller, flaccid and sluggish, would so regard it, but to George it was sheer delight. The alders were felled easily because they were young and their green and grey mottled bark, beautiful as the skin of snakes, concealed a soft, sappy wood. They reeled under the blows, groaned, swung drunkenly and spun earthwards. With bent and twisted branches they throbbed for a moment like living things feeling the agonies of death, and came to rest. The giant Douglas firs were no such easy game. Their corrugated trunks, fluted from base to summit, symmetrical as Corinthian columns, soared up to the sky and spread branches like great dark and velvety fans against the leaden sky. Against these, even the axe lost sense of power: it became a pigmy tool wielded by a pigmy hewer. For these are the mighty ones of the bush, the aged fathers of the forest. They had looked upon the valley through the centuries. Fire had not destroyed them, nor the wind that tore at them, nor yet the silver-frost that weighed their outspread members with tons of frozen water, until they shone, silver bright, like trees of glass. They had conquered the elements and now came man to lay them low.

The open sky, the chasing clouds, pure and sane employment, while over the river and flung along the Eastern Sky lived the mountain range, eternally white and silent – these peaks helped toward a better adjustment of the value and importance of things and bring us a little nearer to the eternal truths.

Winter had gone from the valley; the miracle of spring was at hand. After his long absence the sun, benignly warm, smiled out of a pale-blue sky like a friend returned. The valley washed and nourished by the rains, sparkled in the sunshine. The whole land was emerald green. And the broad river lay like a silver scythe upon the floor of the valley. George described this annual miracle, the eternal cycle of the years; life out of death; beauty out of desolation, through the centuries, through the aeons.

*The great trees of the bush, they knew it too. The sap had risen in them and a new recording ring, unseen, encircled each rugged trunk. The odours of the forest multiply. It is the quickening to life, a universal burgeoning in the Valley, and beyond the Valley, in the bush. The mighty firs put forth the shrill green of their spring foliage; vividly it stands out against the somber green of the forest's winter dress. The forest becomes a vast cathedral of many aisles whose pillars are those giant trees that soar straight up with interlocking branches. A Gothic cathedral, more splendid than any made by man, these groves that were God's first temples.*

For months he toiled on the land with axe and dynamite and fire, his jeans no longer spick and span. The bright blueness had faded. The elk-hide boots into which he thrust his trousers were darkened and scratched. His once smart Homburg hat shapeless, drooping and peppered with cigarette holes, burnt to let the air in.

Walking back from the store one day he struck up a friendship with Old Man Dunn. There is no known resident of the time that fits this character but Godwin makes him easily believable. There was however a Reverend Alexander Dunn and his wife Annie. Early in 1914 at the height of his journal jottings Godwin wrote a long poem in iambic metre titled "Sir Patrick Donald Herbert Dunn". In the poem he writes about coal miners and a strike quelled by the militia. This is written a few months after the infamous Nanaimo coal strike ended. Godwin's Dunn may well have been a reference to James Dunn the Vancouver Island coal baron and former premier of the Province rather than the Whonnck churchman.

Dunn, as described in the book "The Eternal Forest" was a burly, bearded, shrewd old man who had started life in the Yorkshire mines at the age of nine. At fifteen he had mastered sufficient Latin to read Virgil. A good brain in a big body. The people of Whonnock called Old Man Dunn the 'Sage'.

Sitting on his doorstep Old Man Dunn had George as a captive audience. *"Man never learns"*, *he complained. "Every time civilized man so-called, settles in a new country he sets about ruining it. He brings all the bad old ideas of the Old World and leaves the best behind. Every time white men enter a new land God gives them another chance."* The old man became more animated. Although Godwin gives these words to Dunn, they well could have been his own. *"Think of it! Think of this country! Here there is everything – an ideal climate, mineral wealth, billions of feet of magnificent timber, great waterways, fertile soil - everything. A race of wise men, settling here, could have made of this country a Garden of Eden. It is the Garden of Eden. And what have they done with it?"*

In the novel George expands on further conversations he had with Old Man Dunn. He also writes about various characters that were their neighbours and the trials and tribulations they experienced. He details with studied perception how European and Asian immigrants were caught in the economic problems of the time. Conflicts between farmers and exploiters, peasants and speculators, and rural and urban economies are all set against the everlasting power of the forest.

He remembers Old Man Dunn complaining.

*The immigrants have handed their heritage over to the grafter, the land-grabber, the commission-snatcher. They've sold themselves to the big corporation which has no soul and is out for profits and more profits. And the politicians? – Riddled with graft!*
*Your starting out to make a home out of the bush,"* he told George. *"You look forward to seeing a return for your work and for your investment. If you make this place your permanent home, you will raise children here. British children, Canadian-born they will be. Well, what are your prospects?"* George thought he had overlooked one factor – work. If one worked one would be bound to make good. *"I know what you are thinking,"* said the old man, *"you are thinking that you will win through by hard work – that hard work always has its reward. Well I hope you do.*

The clearing became a clutter of felled alders, felled with good will but without method.

George needed help and turned to the big Swede, Johansson, [another apparent Godwin character] who was always ready to help a neighbour. He had discovered the hard fact that the felling of a tree is the least part of the labour of land-clearing.* There remained the stump and the felled tree itself and the tenacious roots of the undergrowth. Johansson came over and told him that the big stumps would need blasting powder. George told Johansson he had tried that with an enormous fir stump using half a box of dynamite sticks, but all it had done was shoot away all the loose heavy soil and left the root intact. Johansson took the long-handled shovel and dug out the dirt from around the splayed roots. He worked like a man digging for gold.

He explained how you could then see the lie of the roots. He took the double-bitted axe, examined the two blades and told George that you should always keep one blade for falling and the other for chopping roots in the ground. That way you got a blade without nicks, one you could keep good and sharp on the stone. He sent the steel into the great root prongs, cutting them across. When half cut the powder would do the rest.

---

* Godwin describes the felled trees as alders which is as it would have been because the first growth firs had been cleared in earlier years. Nevertheless the stumps of those great firs would have remained to be cleared. Earlier he had described the difficulty in felling the great cedars but this may not have been necessary on his own land that had been commercially logged.

The Swede took the two sticks that were left. He dug down into the heart of the root, tunneling narrow shafts under the great stump. He fixed the shining cylinder of the detonator to the fuse wire, nipping the end with his teeth. He cut the fat oily sticks of blasting powder in two, and placed, in all, four charges in his tunnel ends. The real secret was to tamp down good and hard. *"Get air around the stick and you don't git no explosion to count."* The Swede told George.

He tamped the soft earth with a pole of vine-maple, adding shovelful by shovelful until he had filled in his holes, leaving only the fuse ends exposed. He lit the four fuses and the two of them scrambled back to the shelter of a big fir shouting "Fire! Fire!" As they ran a ball of smoke puffed up; the explosion came with a rendering boom; from the shattered stump a shower of debris sang through the foliage. *"Git fire in that hole and she will burn herself out."* He had accomplished within an hour what had baffled George for weeks.

A persistent prodigious writer nothing stopped George from putting pen to paper. Numerous jottings and poems litter his journal. In December one of these "The Academic Dreamer" was published in the Vancouver Daily World (Dec 16, 1913, 2-5).

*You're an academic dreamer, let me tell you*
*good and straight,*
*You spend your life in dreams that don't*
*come true;*
*Why don't you collar hold of life and leave*
*those things to Fate.*
*You'll be a great deal richer if you do.*

44

*I tell you, life's a compromise; just take*
*things as they are.*
*Quit dreams and see things as we others do;*
*Quit all this crazing hitching of your wagon*
*to a star.*
*This dreaming of a dream that can't come*
*true.*
*I'm an academic dreamer? Well, I'm happy in*
*my dream;*
*All your talk of life and wealth just leave me*
*cold;*
*There's something rather low in it, there's*
*something rather mean*
*There's finer things in life than grabbing*
*gold.*
*I'm in that small minority that's looking for*
*the dawn,*
*And it's little that I care for all you say;*
*The East is waxing crimson with the*
*streamers of the morn,*
*And in the dark I'm dreaming of the day.*

[Two changes from the version in his journal
are the spacing and in line four "a damn site richer"
is replaced by " a great deal richer". Perhaps the
editor was a little prudish.]

That same month George must have visited
Stanley Park and found the grave of Pauline
Johnson, the noted Canadian writer and performer
with an international reputation. Johnson was of
mixed Mohawk and English heritage who in her
writings helped create a distinct Canadian
literature and in her stage performances wearing
native costume emphasized her aboriginal
heritage. In 1909 she retired to Vancouver where

45

she died of breast cancer in March 1913. Her ashes were scattered in Stanley Park near Siwash Rock.

Godwin refers to her memorial stone in a short poem he included in his Journal in December from which a few lines are taken as follows.

*She sleeps while o'er her weeping*
*The tall fir trees are keeping*
*Guard o'er her lasting sleep.*
*A stone on the ground disclosing*
*The place of her last reposing,*
*...*
*Where the Siwash Rock is keeping*
*Watch o'er her lasting sleep.*

Throughout the winter of 1913-1914 George wrote several pieces for his journal and one more was published in the Vancouver Daily World (Feb 6, 1914 , 17-4) The Ballad of Burnaby Jail. Clearly based on Oscar Wilde's Ballad of Reading Gaol, a lengthy poem written in 1897 on Wilde's release from gaol where, during his incarceration, a hanging had taken place. The theme of the poem is the death penalty whereas in Godwin's shorter ballad the theme is mistreatment of a prisoner. In his journal Godwin uses the English Gaol but the Vancouver Daily World preferred Jail.

*The Ballad of Burnaby Jail*

*In Burnaby there is a jail*
*And on someone lies the stain*
*Of human blood, for in that jail*
*A miner lad was slain:*
*Was left untended there to die*
*Upon a bed of pain.*

*He did not die, as some men do,*
*Choked by the deadly gas:*
*He was not hauled up from the pit*
*A scorched and blackened mass.*
*In jail he lay, where night and day*
*He heard the warders pass.*

*He heard them tread with feet of lead*
*Upon the prison floor*
*Both day and night, without respite,*
*His agony he bore.*
*And there he died, who had defied*
*Majestic man-made law.*

*Three hopeless days of suffering*
*Three nights of endless gloom*
*He lay and waited silently*
*Within his prison tomb:*
*Waited for those that never came-*
*'Twas thus they sealed his doom.*

*He saw the sun glance fitfully*
*Along the prison wall:*
*His memory bore him swiftly*
*To the days beyond recall:*
*He saw the dark of even come,*
*The final darkness fall.*

*No doctor came to tend him;*
*No woman raised his head-*
*Only the prison guard was  there,*
*Standing behind his bed*
*Or pacing along the prison floor*
*Pacing with feet of lead.*

*The friends who sought to comfort him:*

*His father, grey with years*
*They turned away, that cursed day,*
*Unmoved by parent's tears-*
*Left him without the prison gate*
*Haunted by nameless fears.*

*And all should know that this was so,*
*"A man was murdered there";*
*A man was left to wilt away*
*In foetid prison air:*
*For two and seventy hours was left*
*Without a doctor's care.*

*For he who fight for God-given rights*
*Must suffer at man's hands*
*And he who scorns the right of might*
*They bind in iron bands:*
*And all should know that this is so*
*In this and other lands.*

*In Burnaby there is a jail*
*And on someone lies the stain*
*Of human blood, for in that jail*
*A miner lad was slain:*
*Was left untended there to die*
*Upon a bed of pain.*

[In neither the version in his journal or in the Vancouver World is iambic metre rigorously observed. For example in the second line of the first and last verses of the poem and on three occasions in verses five and six, the metre fails.]

George describes the arduous trials of the grindingly difficult life of the homesteader in such compelling detail that it must surely illustrate the problems faced by the young couple themselves.

The many aspects of that life, the loneliness, the drudgery of daily survival and the inevitable struggle to create income are brought to the reader in stories of the "Newcomer" and his wife. In retelling these episodes from "The Eternal Forrest" they must surely delineate much of the life George and Dorothy faced in their struggle to survive.

*We kept mainly to ourselves. We had cleared about half an acre and planted red clover. The idea was to plough it in the next year and plant potatoes. I hired myself out for whatever work I could find. Sometimes for a few days at the gravel pit, loading wagons for the teams. Once I got work away back in the bush. It was so far back that I would set out while it was still night, with the moon to light the way along silent, ghostly trails in the bush. I carried a lard pail containing lunch: big sandwiches, a screw of salt and apples. It was night when I came back from the shadow of the trees. No more grand living, no more long evenings around the fire. The small patch of brush had by now eaten up our little capital, consumed it insidiously, a bit here for blasting powder, a bit there to pay the Store's bills. Tools, lumber for the chicken houses, haulage up the steep and slippery trail from the river. One thing and another. It was all gone.*

George tried to find work. He preferred it on a contract basis, the more you worked at it, the more money you earned. He felt that wages somehow deadened a person, nobody ought to be paid by the hour. It should be abolished. It ought to be money for work: more work, more money. That would fix the slackers.

A little lady whose husband had a bad heart asked him to cut wood at two dollars a rick, about half a cord, the wood to be delivered. He set out with his dog, Peter, a big, pure-white collie who lollopped ahead, turning round every now and again to wave his fan-like tail and then scamper off into the bush, sniffing, hunting chipmunks: a happy dog. George would walk behind, striding along, lard pail in hand and across his shoulder the springy six foot blade of his crosscut saw. The lard pail in which he carried his lunch was probably made of tin. A cheap container since only the lard was paid for on purchase and the pail was free. The lard rendered from pig fat was used in cooking, baking and frying. Some ceramic pails in North America had painted motifs often depicting native Indian scenes. What memories he reported of that time.

*Long days in the silence of the bush, sawing wood. Perfect stillness everywhere. Beauty all around. A symphony in greens and browns. And the smells! Scents of the aged earth. Moist, living smells that touched the nerves and evoked emotions that belonged to a time long, long ago. And there was life in the bush: teeming life. The stillness was broken only by the unexpected sound of falling twigs and the slow drip of water. A nervous chipmunk, scuttling with the staccato jerks of an automaton, brush waving, along some rotten tree stump, peering inquisitively from the tangle of the forest floor. Holding beech nuts in tiny paws, cracking shells with incredible cleverness. Marvellous strength of canny teeth.*

He took half an hour's rest for lunch, and mental calculations. How many more sections of that tree could be sawn before darkness fell on the bush. Peter looking on, head cocked, awaiting his share, never disappointed. No word spoken, true companionship, perfect confidence on either side.

As the day wore on the piles of split wood by the trailside stacked in ricks, each eight foot by four would grow. Then, as the shadows deepened, the long trudge back to the clearing and the yellow house with smoking chimney to his patient waiting wife. Perhaps eight dollars earned. Eight dollars!

When they arrived in Whonnock Dorothy knew nothing of the management of a house. She had never cooked a meal, never swept a room, never washed so much as a handkerchief. In the first two years she learnt much. Later when George came home the table would be set, the kettle on the stove would be spurting out its homely plume of steam and the smell of cooking food pervaded the warm, cosy kitchen. Dorothy was often silent because in her own department she liked to do everything in her own way. But George remembered that as she would set the meal before him and take her own seat she looked tired. *"A heroic woman without heroics; prosaic, unimaginative, matter-of-fact, but hardened by a vein of unsuspected steel. "*

For supper bread: a cottage loaf with head awry, crisp and brown and light. She had taught herself to bake. Another woman would have gone breezily to a neighbour and borrowed in an hour the other's experience of years. Not so this woman. She bought a book and taught herself. Failure came before success. There was salmon. There was so much salmon on the plate that must be eaten. Meat

51

was a luxury beyond them. Salmon! How they sickened at the repetition of that dish. But see what she could make of it, throughout the long silent day, thinking how she could make a sustaining meal. There would be white sauce and the fish transformed from that familiar flaky pink monotony to a French delicacy.

George's descriptions of the hard life that the wives of homesteaders faced on a daily grind are so compelling that they must have been taken from personal experiences or examples provided by others in the valley.

However, evidence appears to confirm that Dorothy never did come to accept life in Whonnock on this small isolated plot far from the city. Within months she was anxious to return home, though George remained keen to make a go of it. The book suggests that their second child was born in Whonnock but this is not so. Monica was born in Ireland. Nevertheless the constant battle the women faced in trying to keep the home clean and the children and their parents as presentable as possible is well described by Godwin.

*One evening she sighed. "If only I had a washing machine." She looked tired. Her hair was not groomed. She had no corsets on and the big apron made her look shapeless. My eyes rested on her hands. Small hands they were, with fingers scarred by a hundred minute intersecting lines. Work-coarsened hands with ill-tended nails. A washing machine!*
*I went to the pine-wood dresser, picked up the old German beer-mug, relic of the days when I was a realschule student. I gave it a shake by the*

*handle. Only ten cents in the bank, but I would have the money for sawing wood soon.*

*"How much would one of those things cost?" I asked.*

*She knew that, of course, knew precisely the make she wanted and why. " You see with these things you simply heat your water, dump it in with soft soap, bundle the dirty clothes in after, and work the handle to and fro. It saves so much stooping. And we could get one on credit."*

Then there was the constant need for water, at first carried in a bucket from the nearest stream. There was a need to dig a well, but how could one man do that? He would have had to pay a man to work with him. He would be down ten feet and couldn't throw the dirt up any higher and would probably have had to go down another twenty feet! He would need help.

Dorothy loved the Saturday Evening Post as she read the weekly serial. It needed ten cents from the bank. George was glad she suggested taking the money from the bank. He didn't want to suggest it, though he enjoyed the news from the outside world. It was her quiet way – to ask for herself what she wanted for him. What time had she for reading? In the evenings there was mending to do. By nine her head would tilt forward in her chair, her mouth relax and she would fall asleep. That winter, worn with work and care, her first-born came due.

*Snow was on the ground when Bob England brought his sled up the hill with the chestnut team. The horses slipped in the mush. It was the only way we could get Dorothy down. She could not walk neither could she climb into the rig. Bob put straw on the sled and my wife huddled upon it, a little woman with wide open startled eyes. Twice on the downward trail it seemed that catastrophe must overwhelm. The following sled swung round on the soft snow and collided with a tree stump. But she did not cry out. She merely clutched with her little work-worn hands; her patient face blanched a little. A week later, down at the hospital at Sapperton, her baby was born. A boy.*

*Dorothy came back from Sapperton at the end of a full month. Our first child had gone hard with her and her labour had been long and exhausting. Bob England was waiting at the depot with his rig to take her back up the steep trail to the new clearing. I watched as she carried the baby in her arms, a white bundle above which her oval face showed. Her eyes seemed bigger, bluer. She was not quite the same woman now as the one who went down the steep hill precariously on the swaying sled. Maternity had changed her. Suffering seemed to have set a sign upon her: Patient, she looked and very gentle. She bent her head to look into the shawl and drew aside the covering to show me a tiny pink face and a clenched hand no bigger than a shell.*

*I helped her climb into the high rig and handed up to her the white, woolly bundle. All the way up the hill she kept peeping into that nest of warm wool, glancing shyly at Bob England on the front seat beside her, turning back to her baby.*

Dorothy went to Sapperton for the birth of her baby. She would have been taken down to the station and traveled by train to Port Coquitlam and the branch line to New Westminster, with Sapperton having its own station. The Women's

Hospital of New Westminster had amalgamated with the Royal Columbian Hospital in 1901 in the building originally built in 1889. The main hospital moved to an expanded new wing in 1912 so it is probable that Eric was born in the 1889 handsome three-storey building with pleasant landscaped gardens in Sapperton.

Everything would have been made ready for her homecoming. A great fire blazing from the open fireplace where great gnarled prongs of fir-root spurted vivid flames from resinous deposits. She would have been very tired and for the first time since their marriage she would have been content for him to wait upon her. She lay back, the baby propped on cushions beside her. George brought the meal from the kitchen on a tray and there, beside the great fire, the baby by them, they ate simple food. He writes he made a special omelette, *"Omelette Supreme à la Whonnock"*. Scads of butter with a secret. Water instead of milk!

*She agreed languidly that it was good. The warmth of the roaring fire coming after the forty-mile journey had wearied her. I thought she was not so glad to be back as I was to have her back. The baby stirred. The tiny shell of a hand emerged from the swaddling clothes and the shell dissolved into a pink, five-pointed star. A thin, puling wail came from the bundle, which stirred vigorously, then the wail changed with startling suddenness into a vigorous bellow. My wife leaned forward and feeling her already familiar hands about him, the baby turned to a peevish hunger whimper. To me it was a marvel: the woman and the child. My woman, my child. I sat watching with awed eyes as my wife suckled our firstborn. The baby lay cupped in the crook of one arm. My wife opened her loose blouse and lifting her full breast with her free hand, drew the baby towards it. My son burrowed into the white, firm flesh, groping for the nipple, found it and drew it into his sucking mouth. My wife winced, it hurt the doctor had told her to use alum to harden the nipples. But it hurts she said.*

For the women of such settlements as Whonnock, maternity meant sacrifice. The bearing of a child was only the beginning. Thereafter the mothers of the settlement had to be all things to their babies. And at the same time they must do all the work of the little homes where civilization had brought none of its amenities. The men had still to be fed, and there was washing, always washing, to be seen to. Days were long, but not long enough to complete all the tasks of the settlers' wives who had about them growing families. The housework of the city woman was made up of what were, to the wives of the settlers, minor chores of the day. There was no Chinese laundry for the settlers' wife, no telephone for the ordering of groceries. There was no Ford van to call for the orders, no baker to deliver bread.

They must do everything themselves. So, too often, comely women faded and their backs took on an unseemly curve from plucking crying children from cots and carrying them as they go about their kitchens, incessant crying having made physical discomfort and strain a relief for maddened nerves.

George describes how his wife, now, in addition to the cooking, cleaning, washing and

56

sewing, she had the baby to tend. Every four hours he had to be suckled. His washing alone doubled the work. He cried at night and she had not the heart to wake her husband as he slept through such noise as that. The washing machine did not materialize as the extra fees at the hospital had swallowed up any contract money. Numberless napkins were washed day by day by hand. Dorothy, as other mothers, stooped over the corrugated washing board, hair in her eyes, arms working vigorously, face moist with sweat. A flapping line of washing fluttering in the clearing. The baby slept well his milk agreeing with him. They had named him Eric. He slept all morning beside the stump that was like a sentinel; in the shade of the alders his little basket, a laundry basket, was set. And when he awoke and uttered impatient cries, there she was at his side, wiping her wet hands upon her pinafore, unbuttoning her dress.

When Eric had learned to crawl they would put him down in the slashing to feel about for himself. He was a vigorous child and scuttled over the ground on all fours with a sideways movement. They listened to him chortling. They were so proud of him. Then one day when he was able to walk he disappeared. Dorothy had put him out while she washed the bed linen, a heavy task that used up all her strength. And when she came out he had gone. She did not panic at first because there was a chance that he had gone right over to the further side where George was hewing timber. But he had not, and together they rushed madly about. Calling, calling, calling. The baby had wandered off into the bush, over the tangled brush he must have gone, picking the white wood-anemones, burbling to himself. And it was near evening. They sent for help in searching. Terror now had the mother in its grasp. She raised her skirt, and ran forward calling, calling, calling. And thus calling, she stumbled over something, soft and white, in the dim light of the bush. It was her baby, head resting on chubby arm, asleep, unhurt. After that they put a little bell upon him. And at such times as he was out and about the clearing George would stop his work, sawing, felling, building up great fires. To listen and check, and then back to work. George fashioned a little cart on rockers to keep the little fellow amused in one place. It was made of cedar with a little seat and two joy-sticks for the youngster to hold on by.

The coming of the baby had stiffened their backs. There was no turning back now. But there seemed little prospect of making a living off those few acres, even when they had been finally won from the bush, cultivated, and brought into bearing. George was slowly coming to see that, whatever they did, there was no decent living to be made upon the place. First of all, there was insufficient acreage. Then the lay of the land, sloping steeply towards the river below, although it looked to the south, was too steep for practical purposes. Then again, as he well knew from going among the neighbours, only two white settlers in the whole of the settlement were making a living from their land. They had to consider trying to sell the property. But where would they go if they did sell? At least they had a roof over their heads.

For all their problems and grumbles George had come to love the bush, to know every detail, and every varying mood of the scene across the valley with the wide and tranquil river. He knew exactly how Mount Baker gleamed when a faint haze hung over the valley. It was like a floating island in the sky at those times. It was not hard to see it as a fairy castle, set in the clouds; its white, conical head was easily conjured into a turret of ivory.

They talked over their future many times. And, as is often the case, advanced not one step towards a solution of the central problem, the education their son and the founding of a secure future. In some way they both felt that they had been cheated. Certainly they had been deluded, listening to the bland talk of the Vancouver real estate men, reading their lying literature which made ranching in the valley appear as a picnic in the garden of the world.

George had wild schemes, he could be a doctor or they could live in America. Grow oranges in California, sun, glorious climate, easy money – you simply waited until the oranges were ripe and pulled them off the trees and packed them! But Dorothy was very wise. It was certainly true that she never got enthusiastic but she had that abiding quality of seeing a thing through, and keeping on track as well. Doctoring, orange growing – there had been so many schemes to escape from the penury and drudgery of life in Whonnock. They came to nothing.

In the German beer-mug that acted as their bank there was money in it, or there was no money. They lived from hand to mouth and once, for a month, they had no meat. They lived then chiefly on bread and potato soup. The subscription to the newspaper ran out and they had to borrow from neighbours. There were times when money seemed to have disappeared from the valley altogether. There was occasional work, but the hirer would offer apples, potatoes or milk in exchange. So, one way and another they contrived to live, but it was a poor enough living and very different from the one they had expected. At the end of their third year the land had been slashed and five acres cleared and under cultivation.

This is where the book entirely diverts from a historical record of Godwin's time in Whonnock. We know that the second daughter was born in Belfast, not in British Columbia. As Dorothy became less and less happy with their situation, probably doubly worsened by the knowledge that she expected a second child. Though George was anxious not to seem a failure he wanted to stay. Dorothy must have been adamant and returned to her parents in Ireland. The original starkness of the yellow house against the green of the bush had been toned by weather to a dull grey. Flower beds had been marked out with the smaller boulders gathered while clearing; in summer, flowers adorned the place: simple flowers, such as petunias, stock, begonias, pansies and Canterbury bells. Sitting together on the veranda in the evening they looked out at the beginnings of a ranch, and it filled them with a sense of triumph, the sober sense of triumph that comes only after much toil and many fears of failure.

In the evenings when the air stood still they would take their chairs and sit in the open. Below the valley lay in shadow, purple in the half light of evening; the river, seen dimly, leaden-hued. Sometimes a cannery boat would pulse upstream.

The sound of its engine like a fast heart beat, its headlight like a luminous fly in steady flight.

The hardships, the lack of money and with little improvement in sight George begins to refer more and more to the strife that grew between the different ethnic immigrants and with the original native inhabitants of the coast. In the *Eternal Forest* George draws attention to these issues in the way prices were cut, challenges occurred between the city and rural communities and the money grabbing and deceit of the speculators and land agents. These events are almost certainly brought to mind from similar things that happened to George and his wife as they found it harder and harder to survive and their eventual decision to sell up and return to Europe.

*Before going inside one evening my wife had asked if I had got the job of taking boulders off the Woods place. The question released all my fears and frustrations that, as I recall, came out something akin to this.*

*"No. They hired those two Hindus from the back. They work together as a team for five dollars a day. Of course Mrs W. was very nice about it, but it does make one a bit sick when even the white people here don't stick together."*

*"Personally", said Dorothy, "I can't see why they don't prohibit all coloured people coming into the Province. They only take the bread out of our mouths."*

*"I know. By the way, I'm selling all the hens – the whole lot of them."*

*"You're not! All those pedigreed Leghorns, and when they are laying so well?"*

"Well, I am. I got a cheque from the egg-dealer at Sapperton this evening – didn't mean to tell you till morning as a matter of fact. We got nineteen cents a dozen for the last consignment."

"Nineteen cents?"

"Yes, so you see its sheer waste of time to keep the damn things."

"I do think it's disgusting. I suppose it's those Chinese eggs."

"Precisely. In this country it's Chinaman, Japanese, Hindus and Swedes, Italians, Norwegians, every other race – anything but the Anglo-Saxon."

"Yes, and the white men who take the money are the commission snatchers."

"And the gentlemen from across the border with there get rich-quick schemes."

"Perhaps it would have been better if we had cleared out when you wanted to. We can't complain that we weren't warned – old Mr Dunn told us pretty plainly that it was hopeless.

George turned to making chicken crates from cedar slats and had decided to sell the whole damn lot of his birds. Selling to a Chinese dealer, because he gave the best price. He had come to the conclusion that a man was a bloody fool to settle in the valley. But somehow he'd come to like it.

The country was all right, it was the way it was run that was all wrong. They made the odds too difficult for the small man. He had to compete with Orientals and was fleeced by the booms from which he got nothing but land at crazy prices. The big companies squeezed him, to say nothing of the freight rates which swallowed up most of the mangy profits. It was a fine land for everybody but the producer. Not like that in Denmark, and the French and Belgian peasants were better off.

The prospect of selling the homestead made George and Dorothy deliriously happy. They dreamed of a little place in Sussex or Devon, of new clothes that neither of them had had for three years, of a hot bath every day, newspapers and journals, books, theatre and dances!

The man came to assess the property but as soon as George saw him he said :

*"Sorry, nothing doing." Dorothy promptly interjected with consternation in her great eyes, "What do you mean, 'nothing doing?' If he has the money, what does it matter, if he is Japanese? We are leaving the country."*
*But that was how I felt about it. It would have been confoundedly inconsistent. For two years or more I had argued that it should be a white man's country. How could I sell my place just to leave – to a Japanese?*
*Dorothy merely shrugged her shoulders and disappeared into the house. I saw by the heaving of her shoulders that she was struck down by a bitter disappointment. I followed her into the kitchen where, mechanically, she was adjusting the washing machine. I noticed her fingers, calloused, stained with much immersion in greasy water. I saw the little nails, broken and scored with black lines. I knew from that heaving of her shoulders that she was crying with disappointment.*
*Why, after all, inconvenience myself for a mere abstract principle? What difference would my paltry stand make when the Japanese were buying*

63

*land in the Valley every day? The argument went on inside me as I stood there watching my wife's back.*

*But if everybody made a stand against these Orientals, then the Valley would not be going to the dogs. There would be work for all and decent prices for produce. Still, how utterly impossible for one man to make a stand! One's wife and children came first. Of course they did! Would the children one day applaud their father for committing a quixotic act that compromised their future? I wanted the boy to have an English education. To stand thus on principle was perhaps doing him out of the chance of one.*

George turned the matter over in his mind and realized that it had always been like that in the past. It had been like that when he had everything set to run away from St Lawrence School. It had been the same old thing when he became engaged. True, he had a comfortable set of chambers to which he might easily have taken a bride. But he had refused to take the easy way, because it was the easy way: it had seemed like not playing the game by the woman he loved. To give it all up and set out for Canada, to start clear and make a home – that had seemed the right thing, perversely, because it was the hard thing. Was it just cussedness, obstinacy? Who, in God's name, would thank him for putting his puny carcass in the way of the Japanese invasion? Nobody! For the good and sufficient reason that nobody cared!

In the novel George refers to them returning to the routine of their lives on the fringe of the bush, and putting aside the dream of home. This may have been the time that Dorothy had finally had enough and planned to return to Ireland. The sudden prospect of leaving made George alive to what the bush really meant. It got hold of you and made you think, it gave you your place in the universe, taught you the significance of man; it whispered of God.

It was astonishing, to think of it. London: everybody eating and drinking, wearing out clothes, millions of them, living in houses of bricks and mortar, consuming, taking from the earth. And just following professions and jobs which had sprung up like fungi. Giving nothing back to the soil. The whole population of the world, all the teeming millions that eat and eat and wear out and consume, the moneychangers, banks, insurance offices, commission-men, middle-men, all the white-collar people, just feeding off the man whose sweat produces the wherewithal of existence. The richest men were those furthest from the soil. The most artificial of all the artificial types that civilization had produced were the money-changers. The more useful your work is, the less you get paid, and the reverse.

When the money gave out George turned to work with the road gang on Baker Road. After all, anyone could labour, given ordinary strength. It didn't require knowledge. There was no technique to a pick and shovel. That was wrong, of course. Even manual work required skill. Amazing discovery! Yes, there is technique to the simplest manual action. There is no unskilled work. There are merely unskilled workers. At first George grasped the pick and swung it high, lustily, eager to show his strength. And that was all wrong. There was gravity, friend gravity, which helped. One merely raised one's pick and let it drop. No need of an arduous downward tug: gravity did that, the road surface split under the steel nose with no other force than the weight of the unwieldy tool. Shovels too. Tools of infinite variety. What ease to show when the edge of the tool was sharp! What misery, when it curled like a lettuce! One learnt. Slowly, laboriously. But one learnt.

He took his lunch alone, clambering a little into the bush. He took with him a book, it was *Elia*, it took him back, as did no other book, to England, to that other life, that other world, then no more real than a tale remembered.

Looking down to the low rich land beside the river where a patterned market garden displayed its ordered comeliness. A blue-robed figure beneath a great straw hat moved along the green rows, stooping to pluck a lurking weed, marking each growing thing with patient almond eyes. Three times he had sown turnip seed, and three times the fly had consumed the tender leaves. But by the fourth sowing the fly was gone, the crop survived germination, and the first thrust from dark to light. Now it was growing apace. There was a fine crop. But the white settlers, cursing the blight, sowed only once. Later they bought from the Chinaman because he alone had turnips for sale. The white men worked upon the new roads, eating up the government grants like locusts. Defeated men they were, for they could not make a living from their land. They thought in wages, sometimes going up into the mountains of the mainland to sweat in the smelting works at Trail or Kaslo, coming back to their little ranches with their wages. But more often selling out and moving into the city.

And then Old Man Dunn added to the homesickness. He and his wife were going home to Yorkshire!

The valley and the bush were beautiful but George lived in the shadows. For George the horror of failing to provide was a daily torture which rose to desperate fear at times. With Dorothy there was always the fear of adding to the problem. The idea of another child haunted her. To live again those long and weary months of physical discomfort, to face again the pangs of labour, the months and years of toil for the baby and the child.

Then one day, after lifting a weighty log, George spat up blood. A three mile walk along the CPR tracks after work to the doctor. The rail tracks were used as a walking path to go east or west. The local roads were muddy in winter and dusty in summer and in need of constant repair. He was told that nine out of ten people had tubercular lesions on their lungs. They probably got it before they turned five, and their untainted young blood fights off the fungous parasite. The lung is damaged and eaten into but it heals. The process is called calcification. In most cases those early-healed lesions never break down. Sometimes they do. George's had. Some strain put upon the system which was too great for it. A handshake, a kindly word. Malt, rest, no strain. Three dollars – a day's work, and three miles back to the ranch.

Should he tell his wife? There was no money. If he gave up manual work without explanation she would think him a quitter. Here the book deviates from reality, perhaps to add reason for George quitting the bush and returning to England or for

Dorothy insisting that she return to Belfast for the birth of her second child, a daughter, in January 1916. They probably left Whonnock in the fall of 1915. The daughter was born in Belfast, the birth certificate listing George as the father living in the Temple in London, though recording the birth from Garrdha Knock (Garden Hill) Belfast, probably the home of his in-laws.

*I moved to the house, an empty man. Creeping along the veranda, I peered through the bedroom window. In the great bed she lay, the baby in the crook of her arm. Her head was thrown back, her gentle mouth slightly opened. Weariness sat, like the insignia of her abiding steadfastness, on her brow. Then at a slight noise the baby moved, raised a round head, releasing the breast from which she fed. She fixed two blue, incurious eyes upon the face at the window. A spray of milk, as from a fairy fountain, spurted upon the tiny face.*
*It was time to sell, time to go home.*

Now George moved into the world of unscrupulous real estate agents, the promise of a sale, but never forthcoming. He arrived in Vancouver in a blaze of August sun that baked the city. At the top of Granville Street he paused to mop his sweating face. He wore the old overalls in which he worked about his place. They were sun and rain faded, patched here and there, and threadbare. On Hastings Street he stood before a large plate glass window across which sprawled in self-assertive gold letters the legend:

ANGUS FERGUSON Real Estate: Oil Lands: Insurance: Notary Public.

Ferguson was stout and urbane. He had a round, pink, freckled face, red hair, and beneath two bushy brows a pair of shrewd grey eyes. A slight change came over his face when George stated that he had come to sell, and not to buy, land. The fat man told him there was a bunch of Fergusons in Vancouver and some more in Victoria. An old family. His grandfather had been the first. George had heard stories of Old Man Ferguson and had a clear picture of the old pioneer: a sturdy Scot, hard as nails and dogged as a Highlander is dogged. *

George looked with curiosity at what the third generation of that hardy race had produced, and saw a soft and flabby man, slowly chewing gum and exhaling a sickly odour of the tonsorial parlour. A man with fat, pink hands set off by carefully manicured nails. A man with a taste for flashy ties and a mouth made conspicuous by many gold fillings. Were any of his people still on the land?

*"The land?"* he sneered in a voice of disgust. *"The land's for the easy marks. For the newcomers. No, sir. Give me the city, where there's somphun doin '. Every time. Money to be made. Yep. Money. Sure, I'm out for the dollar. Why not? Ain't everybody out for all he can get? You bet yer."*

---

*There was a Hector Ferguson who had arrived in Haney in 1878 whose grandparents were from Perthshire, but the first white settler in Whonnock in the early 1860s was Robert Robinson who originated from the Shetlands. (Whonnock Notes)

*"Wal, I've listed your ranch, and if anyone can find you a buyer, I'm him".*

George returned by the evening local. Dreams of that little place in Sussex were born again.

Just a year earlier as the war in Europe dragged on, Maple Ridge, the municipality in which Whonnock stood, decided it was to have its own infantry company. Bob England talked George into being involved on behalf of the settlement. If he had had the courage he would have said:

*No thanks. I'm against this war and I'm against all wars. I've been reading Tolstoi. It's merely murder. I'm a pacifist, so put that in your pipe and smoke it. Besides, I like the Germans. So put that in your pipe and see how the mixture smokes.*

But he didn't do anything of the sort. There was no way out. Along with his failure on the land and the call from the "Old Country", it had to be.

# Why Stay We Here?

The life of George Godwin now turns to his enlistment in the army for service in the Great War. This part of his life is told in a remarkable book written and published almost ten years after the war. Again it is told through a third person but almost certainly draws on his personal experiences. The book is a compelling reminder of the tragic physical and psychological miseries of that time. The book *Why Stay We Here* was published at the end of the 1920s and never received the accolade it deserved. It went out of print only to be reissued along with *The Eternal Forest* in the 1990s.

George had already written in his journal about the war as early as October 1914 in a poem with the title "Little Mothers".

*Little grey mother why do you weep*
*There by the hearth where the long shadows creep*
*Their chairs are empty, my sons they are gone*
*Heard ye no laughs at the grey of the dawn?*

*Little grey mother now wipe you your eyes*
*O quicken your heart and stifle your sighs*
*Tis lightly you speak to the woman who bore*
*The sons that are gone to come back nomore.*

*Little grey mother your lot is to wait*
*There by the fire side both early and late*
*Guard you their chairs lest thy sons do return*
*Watch you the fire that so brightly may burn.*

*A stench from the trenches poisons the air*
*The battered, the dead and the dying are there*
*And many odd hundred bloody and torn*
*The sons who answered the bugles at dawn.*

[A fifth and final verse cannot be accurately transcribed from the journal.]

George's first steps on the return to Europe took him to the recruiting office in Sapperton just north of New Westminster. At Sapperton the examining officer declared him *"sound as a bell"* at first, but a few moments later said he could not pass him because of *"that bum shooting eye"*. He told George to go home and wait; *"they'll need you sooner or later."*

Unless the homestead sold he needed a loan to get to Europe. Nobody seemed to care to lend money on land in the Fraser Valley at that time. In the end George wrote he was grateful to an extortionate private lender who advanced him a thousand dollars at twelve percent. At that moment it seemed almost an act of kindness. *"A thousand dollars, two hundred pounds, a slender purse with which to face the journey home."* In the book George describes a journey of the family by train across Canada and then to New York and Liverpool though Dorothy may have left ahead of George with their first born son.

When Dorothy returned she probably left for Ireland from Liverpool by the Irish packet as alluded to in this his second book. George on his return to England *"took the London train. In a toy carriage, drawn by a nursery engine, speeding through tiny fields whose trees were no bigger than big bushes. England had shrunk, become an absurd little land, yet primly beautiful.*\*

The train took him to Paddington arriving in darkness. The great station was a cavern of many echoes, of shadows that came and went in the gloom. *"And in the Temple, 3 Plowden Buildings, that dear, dear familiar place, how changed."* George felt that he had come upon an old and solid friend with a tale of penury and woe.

George described it as:

*A slow business, getting into that war. And little wonder, since it was conducted by lunatics. In Sapperton they had discovered a disqualifying right eye. Now there was nothing right at all.*

*I had completed my training in the Officer's Training Corps. It began with a medical examination, and ended with one. In the three intervening months, so it seemed, the A.1 human machine had become derelict, below even the C. 3 grade. Three months had been long enough for the discouraging revelation that war enthusiasm a day from the guns burnt less fiercely than war enthusiasm five thousand miles from them.*

*The O.T.C. had been the school cadet corps all over again, glorified, redeemed here and there from boredom. As, for instance, by advanced ballistics expounded by a professor (with German bas reliefs to illustrate bow-and-stern air waves and*

---

\* A sentiment that many expatriate British people returning from Canada would express to this day.

*the like) for those who were curious enough to probe the mysteries of flying death.* *

*During the training period, so familiar were uniform, routine of drill and instruction in lecture hall that it was as though one had slipped back into the familiar setting of the old school. In that matter-of-fact atmosphere (so little do sergeant-instructors vary) the Great Moral Issues which had loomed so large as one leant on an axe and meditated in the silences of the bush, dwindled and disappeared. Tolstoi and his teaching went clean out of mind.*

Rejected, George tells us his alter ego took a small room in a side street in Soho. He wore a borrowed suit of checks, having sold his clothes three months before. It was tight under the arms, too short in the legs. He looked like a scarecrow. Conscious of this, he interpreted the looks upon the faces of others, that now and then seemed vaguely hostile, to this absurd appearance. The explanation came later. A girl with a bottle-shouldered youth in khaki threw it over her shoulder as she passed: *"My boy's in khaki. Wot's your girl think of you?"* A pretty little thing, too, with fair hair and wide blue eyes. How happy she was, how proud of her pimply soldier boy!

By then the last of his money was gone. In Canada there had been times when the temptation to write home for financial help was overpowering. But they had never done it. Now it was necessary to surrender. He would have to borrow. Best get it over.

A bearded old uncle stood up in his office, adjusted gold-rimmed glasses and asked. *"A loan?"* *"But why?"* Hospitality, yes. A loan went against the grain. How to explain the case clearly so that this old man would understand? No case could have been clearer. He wanted money because he had none: wanted it, not for himself, but for his wife. He wanted it for her because this thing called the British Empire temporally required his whole time, had for the time taken away freedom to work and earn. And this pink-faced old man was part and parcel of that monstrous entity. He might have stood as its symbol: solid, stolid, hard-headed, obtuse. If he got to France and fought, it was for him, for his wealth, so small a part of which George now desired to borrow. A reasonable request, surely.

George knew he had foregone his home that he had made with his two hands, left wife and children, surrendered liberty, undertaken to obey superior officers, and those set in authority over them in turn, in all things. And undertaken, further, to ignore all personal danger, to accept all bodily risk and, if necessary, die in the process or suffer malnutrition. His wife, who made her sacrifice without protest, and his children, who were too young to know anything about the matter at all, were also partners to this contract. Signed, sealed and delivered.

*And on your part, dear uncle, since contracts are matters of give and take, you will eat less butter than you did and sell your saddle horse for army purposes. But be of good cheer, you will make money. This is one of the peculiar consequences of war against which your philosophy will arm you.*

*Even so, you, too, as patriot, have your duties. Your country, uncle, needs you. At least it needs your money. But it is no more unreasonable with you than with me. Of me it asks youth, home, a warm place in bed beside my wife, the caresses of my children. Perhaps more. So you, good uncle that you are, will buy your War Loan. The interest is your due. Meanwhile, ten pounds is an urgent need.*

His uncle grasped George with avuncular heartiness. *"A loan, my boy? Of course. Nobody appreciates more than I all that you have done, all that you are doing for your King and country."* *Rummaging in his strong box, smiling "Fifty to get on with and more when it's done. Not a word. Not another word. This is not a loan. Merely a partial liquidation of my indebtedness to you, to your generation."*

*Something wrong here, most certainly. Bearded age had missed its cue. My face scarlet, tears of mortification in my eyes, I signed the I.O.U placed before me, gulped my thanks and hurried away from that old man.*

*So this war left one nothing, nothing at all. Not even one's self-respect, one's pride, one's independence.*

The book tells that brother Dick appeared out of nowhere at a most opportune moment. They met in the tea lounge of the Hotel Cecil, where the war was not permitted and all went on as usual. The Cecil Hotel, also known as the Salisbury Hotel, was a grand hotel built in the 1890s. With a splendid Palm Court it stood between the Thames Embankment and the Strand.

A waiter of obvious military age brought tea, set the table before them and moved off, for the first time blessing the affliction of flat feet. Dick knew George wanted a commission so he explained how it could be done. *"Go straight to the Minister, Old Sammy at the Savoy surrounded by chocolate majors. Never mind them shove in. Don't ask for an appointment with the Minister. Breeze right in. A particularly snotty chocolate major will push his silly face out of Sammy's door. Walk in. And now for the important part. He is vain. He is pledged to rise to the patriotic appeal. His reaction will be automatic. He is kind hearted. But vain peacocks aren't in it. Appeal to him for a commission. Tell him it's his well known good heart that has brought you here. Everybody has told you that you would get a square deal from him. We all have to do our bit. Tell him you have come from B.C. to do yours. You want a commission in the C.E.F."*

Dick described as tall and lean in khaki, sporting the thin gold badge of the wounded. George thin, tanned in those absurd checks. How well Dick looked in his uniform! Three stars. A Captain. Wounded at the Somme. A hero. And that ridiculous moustache, though it suited him. *

---

* If indeed Dick was injured at the "Somme" it was probably in the Battle of St Eloi in the spring of 1916. The battle preceded the main Somme offensive and was the introduction of Canadian troops into a baptism of fire in water filled mine craters and shell holes. The battle cost a Canadian loss of 1373 casualties.

And so it proved. True, it took two weeks to get into the presence. True, too, that the chocolate major put up an unexpected resistance as guardian of the door.

True, *sotto voce,* rude remarks were made upon the appearance of the persistent applicant. But the Minister rose to the bait, melted visibly before the flattery. Gave the word. The commission was given, lieutenant in the Canadian Expeditionary Force. Why was George so jubilant? *

*Was it because I was about to close with the hated Hun? No. No. Was it because I was about to receive the King's Commission? No. Was it because the objective that had brought me half way round the world was about to be realized? No, again. I rejoiced because a lieutenant received good pay and a generous allowance for wife and children. Once again, as so often in Whonnock when things seemed desperate I had won a way to bread and butter, had solved the immemorial problem of making a living.*

Fifty pounds would have bought a splendid kit. But there was so much more to do with it. It would draw together beneath one roof, for some time at least, the members of a small divided family. It was to establish a temporary home of sorts and restart the idle wheels of the old domestic machine. And incidentally, it was to provide full service kit for yet another lieutenant: uniform, boots, field glasses, compass and weapon.

---

* By 1916 the Force consisted of 4 battalions and by 1918 had mustered over 600,000, two-thirds of whom served overseas and 50,000 died.

At this point George describes the family united again. How the boy had grown. The baby was puling, tired after the long journey by boat and train (probably from Ireland). The fifty pounds had stretched and stretched, but there were limits. It was a skeleton kit, so unlike the magnificent outfits with which proud parents and relatives were equipping their schoolboys for war. No tailored tunic or 'bespoke' breeches. Weapon, binoculars, compass, they would come later. Enough for the moment that they were together again. A tiny flat with a little bedroom in a Kentish town of narrow streets and low houses. No bed or cot for the baby. But Dorothy pulled out the bottom drawer and it was now a cot. The war seemed quite a long way off. Very, very faintly through the open window came the sound of the sea breaking on the shore. And another sound with it: a low, just audible rumble from across the grey waters of the Channel. The guns.

Long days at the camp, on the square, in the lecture room. Cocktails in the canteen. Shoveling in trenches and taking part in a mock raid on a dark night. Easy enough, pleasant enough in its way. George found it all just a trifle boring. In a letter to Ted Roberts in 1965 George writes of being in camp, not in Kent, but in Seafort on the coast of West Sussex and his family was in Pulborough. He wrote that "*he used to cycle home at weekends* [about 25 miles], *on one side was the Channel on the other ordinary Sussex arable.*" And always the evenings to look forward to. Evenings at home with Dorothy and the children. No need to worry about next month's bread. It was assured. The pay came as promptly as the rations.

Orders for France came on an October day [1916] of wind and rain, with grey clouds a-scud over a dreary waste of Channel. George was to report at once to Sandling Camp a mere mile or two away.*

He was out of the camp in a flash. France at last. It was what one had been preparing for. It was what one had come across Canada, across the Atlantic for. Still to leave family now, to go, when it came to going it wasn't pleasant. The future loomed up darkly with a thousand possibilities, and none of them pleasant.

George described their parting, which must have been like so many others as husbands and fathers left for France.

*We dressed by gaslight. There was so much to say, so short a time for the saying. I glanced at the sleeping baby and passed quietly into the tiny room beyond for a few last minutes with my boy. It might be a last long look. I might never see again this little head of yellow hair, this baby puckered face, this soft sweet mouth. It was not yet four o'clock. I could not wake him. There could be no final smile, no kiss, no wide blue eyes. No close hug, heart of father to heart of son.*

*We sat for breakfast and ate in silence, but our thoughts were everywhere. There was no need of words. Dick came with his sidecar, sounding the horn. Dorothy came with me in the narrow passage.*

---

* West Sandling Camp, sometimes shortened to Sandling, was a First World War camp in Kent and could have been only a mile or two from the "Kentish town" referred to.

*It was Good-bye. I held her close. A last embrace? Who knew? Then let it be long and ardent. But then go quickly, for there is a breaking point. I waved from the pulsating machine. The last impression; a woman standing in a lighted doorway.*

In Dick's sidecar they sped through the darkness to the crowded station. Southampton, and pink-faced lads in khaki, waiting in the cold gloom of great wharf sheds; schoolboys dressed as men, as soldiers, officers, lads with schoolboy faces, graces, airs. Beautifully turned out, they were, with amazing varieties of luxury kit. They seemed to be festooned with leatherware. Beside them the Canadian officers looked like elder brothers. On the boat, black and sinister, a lad with the badge of the Royal Fusiliers on his lapel came up and offered a khaki article from which hung tapes, a patent bullet-proof waistcoat. George turned it down; he was no hero but would have hated to be picked up in it. The youth nodded comprehensively admitting that that was the way he felt, but you couldn't blame mothers for the way they were. He'd have to chuck it overboard.

Three ghastly days in Le Havre in the camp upon the hill. And then the train at last and O'Reilly and Piers, both bound for the same battalion, brothers. O'Reilly taking nothing seriously, with always a droll story in that Canadian drawl that had about it a hint of Dublin. And Piers, slow and whimsical, startling you when you least expected it with a bawdy story; then later, mood changing, talking books, poets. Something lovable about Piers, thin and gaunt and melancholy. At Rouen there was twelve hours of waiting. George writes of O'Reilly and Piers, fellow volunteers, but probably names created from his imagination. The journey he describes is almost certainly the route they took across the English Channel and then by train eastward through Northern France.

*Then on to the transport lines where we sat in the dim light of the Paymaster's office. A whisky bottle stood on the bare table, and each man had a glass; the Paymaster, the guide and the three draft officers, just in. I told myself that this was the front. In half an hour we would go up to the trenches. It seemed impossible.*

*A pleasant man who took life comfortably, this Scottish paymaster. Bland and smiling, with a little trick of sucking in after each observation. It was as though he tasted and savoured his words as he tasted and savoured his whisky.*

*Just what had one expected? That was not easily defined, but one had expected noise, terrific shattering noise. Tenseness. One had come up to the front line braced for it. And there was no noise, only astonishing inaction. Uncanny silence. But behind the calm an old preoccupation. Presently there was to be a battle. The Ridge was to be taken, that low hump that was lost by the sorely-tried troops under Sir Henry Wilson almost a year before.[May 1916] The impending battle lay like a cloud upon them.*

*The interminable talk of the Paymaster came to an end. The guide, a nonchalant lieutenant between whom and the new arrivals was fixed that great gulf that divides those who have been in the line and those about to go in it for the first time, rose. His tunic was soiled and shabby, and on whose arms the battalion badges were an eloquent rain-washed blue.*

82

*We left the village behind and were walking in file along the communication trench, upon the duckboards, stooping now and again to dodge wire. Here was desolation. All sign of green was gone from the landscape. Soon there was only the uniformity of a shell-churned earth an ochreous yellow, or deeper dun. Tree and stumps, here and there, stood like witnesses to man's crimes against the earth and the life thereof, and the sweetness thereof, and the fullness thereof.*

Suddenly, high above an enemy plane, a Red Devil. In that tiny machine, in its cockpit, there was a Teutonic intelligence, keen, fearless, determined. In a moment there was another machine in the sky. Very faintly the roar of the engines came to the little party in the trench. Crackle of machine gun fire. They are engaged. How soon it ended! Higher and higher rose the victorious machine while below it, a fiery comet trailed dense black fumes, the vanquished plane spiraled down and crashed a mile or more away. That is all. The little party proceeded on its way.[x]

After all, there was a war here. The silence was broken.

*"A" Company H.Q. dugout; a mouth in a sandbag face. The guide stooped and disappeared within. We followed in file. It was dark, and the*

---

[x] The term "Le Diable Rouge" or Red Devil was applied to the German flying ace von Richthofen. It is probable that Godwin used it as a pseudonym for any German aircraft rather than specifically von Richthofen.

uneven steps were steep and slippery. The dugout was thirty feet below trench level. The guide pulled aside a rough curtain of sacking, and a tired, handsome face peered out. The Company Commander was sitting sideways at a rough bench upon which were papers, a holster, an empty tin mug and plate with fat-smeared knife and fork. A candle, thrust into a bottleneck, lighted his work and filled the dugout with moving shadows. The guide saluted and announced we three draft officers and passed into the shadows beyond.

The Major greeted us with a slow smile of welcome. Not a man of words, this dignified veteran of the Somme, about whom there is an air of detachment, serenity, remoteness. He is in the war, this man past middle age, but scarcely of it. He indicated the bench and George slumped down beside him. We talked a little; he had a brother in Whonnock. The candle burned steadily. The chicken-wire bunks on which Piers and O'Reilly sat creaked as they listened. Suddenly there was a shattering crash, an ear splitting detonation. A blast of air gushed into the dugout: we were in total darkness. Debris fell from the dugout walls, earth cascading down in little avalanches. We could see nothing, only hear and smell. The stench of spent high-explosives in our nostrils.

In the darkness, calmly, the Major asked if any one was there. A sergeant appeared, torchlight framed a dark and brooding face beneath a forward-tilted helmet. The sergeant rubbed his elbow. He had been blown down the steep steps headfirst. "Coal-box, sir," he explained laconically. "Jerry isn't playing fair this afternoon. It's only four o'clock."

84

*For weeks the Saxons in their trenches, forty yards away, had been taking things easy. But every afternoon around five o'clock the battalion had come to look for the evening hate, a sporadic activity of machine guns, bombs and coal-boxes (large caliber artillery shells) that lasted half an hour or so. But never before a sporting signal: a flippant tattoo of snapping machine-gun fire high overhead in warning.*

*A corporal, rifle slung piloted him on his first duty round explaining that in some places Jerry was only thirty yards away. From the Kellett line, facing to the east, the conformation of the ground was visible, a reach of mud, pitted with craters and shell holes, littered with wire entanglements. A hump like a monstrous slug, Vimy Ridge broke the arc of the eastern skyline. To the south the flanks of Notre Dame de Lorette rose steeply, scarred by abandoned trench works. All that remained of the Bois en Hache were a few totem poles of charred and splintered wood. Trees, once upon a time. [A result of fighting in October 1915] Over this desolation, now lit by a watery sun, the tide of battle had washed backwards and forwards. And would wash again. The coming battle brooded over the trenches and the men in the trenches.*

As a newly fledged officer Godwin described how on his first day he was shown the job of his subordinates.

*Progress was slow because at one part of the trench the duckboards were sunk two feet in yellow mud. We wore thigh gumboots and at every step pulled our legs up out of the sucking mud and let* them sink back in again. We came to a man standing on a fire-step, eyes glued to a periscope. I was asked to take a look. In the periscope I could see a wide section of No Man's Land. There was something hanging there across the enemy's wire. He had lost his way, though it seemed impossible.

"Been there three days," the N.C.O. said. "We can't get him in. Not that it matters much. He's dead. But still...." But still.... No need to say more.

We moved along, the corporal went ahead.

"Keep your head low here, sir, we're open to enfilade fire."

I turned and could see that we were fully exposed to No Man's Land. Across the trench, every few yards, were piled sandbags on beams from side to side. Below curtains of sacking hung. Some protection but not much.

Somewhere over there, among those tangled wires of the enemy's trenches, there was a watching eye. I felt it on the back of my head. Now he was aiming, finger on trigger, eye close to telescopic sight. Any moment. . . But no. We reached the first curtain of sacking and passed beyond. A machine-gun emplacement was revealed. The crew turned round, saluted.

Every inch of that interminable way would have to be retraced, including this stretch within the German sniper's field of vision.

An hour later, the tour nearly done, ploughing slowly through the mud I pulled aside the sacking. A report, sharp as a whip crack, snapped above my head, a wet stinging impact of bullet into sandbag. The corporal pulled me back. The curtain fell to.

"Nearly got you, sir, " said the corporal. "The bastard!"

*What did one do? Officer and N.C.O. Of course this fellow knew infinitely more about the game than me. But I wore two stars upon my shoulder straps. They made all the difference, even if mine was a Tommy's tunic, just like the man's beside me.*

*Officers lead, other ranks did what they were told. Impossible to stand here all day. On the other hand, waiting, with his rifle lined on that sacking, was a watchful sniper. What could I do? Angry with myself I was funking it. Funking it on a day when the line was quiet as a Sabbath afternoon. What would I be like when the rough stuff began?*

*"Well, we'll be getting along. Keep well down, sir."*

*My heart throbbed with a sobbing beat against the wall of my chest. Perhaps now? No. Well, then, he is taking extra special care to get me this time. But no. Two more steps, three, four, five. I swallowed a lump in my throat. Of all abominations: to pitch head foremost and die in this polluting mud!*

*The first tour was done. At the dugout, now already wearing homely, I wanted to turn in for a bit, but the Company Commander reminded me I had to submit a Report. I recall it went like something like this.*

*O.C. 'A' Co.*
*Sir,*
*I beg to report as follows (8am – 11pm)*
*Everything quiet.*
*No 3 MG crew report a sniper busy at a point roughly from their emplacement N. 20 or 30 rounds fired.*

*Another sniper is operating at a point so far as I can judge E by SE from MG No2.*

*G Godwin.*

*I thought that was enough, but the Major wanted to know about the wind.*
*"Have you never heard of gas?"*
*I was learning the job.*

In the afternoons, after days of inactivity, when it seemed as though the war had become a matter of alert watchfulness and nothing more, the enemy's evening hate would begin. But always first that friendly warning: the music hall tattoo of the machine gun, facetious, grotesque in this place. [x]

The machine guns traversed the trenches, scattering mud and sand, splintering woodwork, but beyond that did little harm. For that a man well entrenched would scarcely stop from scratching. But the sausages, heavy trench mortar bombs, were another affair. They came sizzling across No Man's Land in a drunken parabola, their sterns waggling. You could watch them as they came. Dodging sausages was a science more easily learned for having played Fives. They gave one time, a sense of direction, so that one could dash for the next traverse and there shelter, crouching down. A little shaking, a ringing in the ears. But nothing worse. But when they exploded, as they sometimes did, right in the trench, there was a hole big enough to house a transport wagon comfortably. Now and

---

[x] The winter of 1916/1917 was largely a waiting game with action put in abeyance by the weather and cold rains.

then, they caught a man unawares; and when that happened, there was little left of him.

Life shared in the dugout was a community life. There were no comforts. There was no privacy. All ate at the narrow bench which was also the Company Commander's office; slept in the two-tiered bunks. And as they ate food which had been hot when it left the battalion kitchen half an hour before, but was hot no longer, rats, scurrying insolently among the beams, scattered dirt upon the food. Sometimes the bread ration ran short.

The tour over the battalion withdrew to the support trenches. Winding along a labyrinth of duck-walled trenches deep in mire, the men breathing heavily, talking but little. They are tired, wet, cold and hungry. The harsh bark of coughing betrayed their slow progress. In the front line dugouts a man might generally stand erect. True enough, there were often inches of water underfoot, but a little ingenuity, a few scrounged Mills bomb boxes and you could contrive a flooring of sorts. Besides, there were the bunks, high above the dirt where, by candlelight, a man might smoke and read in peace. But here the century was no more. These billets would have grieved a cave man. Huddled like a pigmy village in the open, the sandbag hovels, roofed with corrugated iron, are really sties, igloos of mud, kennels no more than four feet high. The men go into them on all fours, like dogs, dragging their equipment with them. They spread their ground sheets, muttering, search for candles, matches. How could a man sleep like this? How could a man clean up? It wasn't to be done. Suffering Christ, it wasn't.

The men went overland to Ablain St. Nazaire to clean up unwashed bodies, to draw from the Q.M. store grey shirts, clean and smelling of the bake-house. There were lice upon these baked shirts, it was true, but they were dead lice and therefore of no account. The bathhouse had canvas walls, duckboard flooring and rows of iron pipes overhead from which hot water, scalding water fell. The place was full of steam and naked men, men with spotty bodies, little sores from scratching, lousy men soon to be cleansed, but soon to be verminous again.

The descriptions of trench life and the rare but welcome relief of rest and washing are such that they must be taken from Godwin's own reminiscences of that time. Even if written some years later the memories must have been burned into his mind.

He relates how he and his comrade climbed from the village of Ablain St Nazaire to the summit of Notre Dame de Lorette. From this eminence on a good day, there was a clear view across the plains to ruined Arras. Vimy to the east seemed to lie far below, though strangely, from Vimy, German eyes looked down upon this other hill. The ground between was hieroglyphed with trench works. Ablain St. Nazaire was a mere pile of grey debris with one large dominating slab – the ruined church. To the north, Liévin and Lens flourished untouched behind the German lines.

Piers, we're told, particularly wanted to find the shrine to Our Lady of Loretto a great place of pilgrimage where, every year, thousands of devout and credulous souls came to beg a boon of the flash plaster lady of the shrine. She was considered almost as great a wonder-worker as the Virgin at Lourdes. They reached the summit and found themselves amid a complete system of abandoned trenches, all fallen in and tufted here and there with coarse grass. Looking down into a collapsed trench from which sprouted tangled rusty wire and coarse grass tufts George stooped and picked up a rusted bayonet and examined it. Then, idly, he kicked a boot that lay, sole upturned, in the mud. It rolled over and there in the gaping mouth was a skeleton foot. The snapped bone remained erect, a little stick, a little splintered tree, but one that would never come to leaf. The shin bone thrust upwards from the sea of mud; yellow it was, like old ivory.

*Mort pour la Patrie. Vive La France! Dulce et decorum est.*

*"How would the Boot have been reported? As dead? Or among the missing? Probably among the missing.*

*In little smudgy type, read through spectacles by a fat, dark woman with a black moustache. Missing. Well, then, there was hope, n'est ce pas? Perhaps he is taken prisoner? Yes, that would be it. A prisoner. Hardship avec les sales Boches, but safe for the duration of the war.*

*Off to church. Dimness; heavy incensed air. And beyond that dimness: God. The good God who had arranged it thus. Candles before the tinsel shrine. The blessed saints protect him! Kneeling there, stout, short of breath, the Boot's mother. Praying, a little fat woman; perspiring, a drab little woman with a black moustache.*

*Praying for the Boot. Waiting patiently for the Boot's return.*

*And then – doubt. Doubt as she waddles through the entresol. Among the missing. Could that mean…..? Impossible! The good God would not allow it.*

*Aye, Boot, perhaps it is like that at home, eh? The good God has forgotten or has He taken you to that paradise of his?*

*Did the Boot hope to rise some day and come together with all those missing bones, that vanished flesh? Do you wait patiently for the White Angel of the Lord to sound his trumpet call across this desolation? And were you afraid at the last, were your toes in the right direction? And who did you call upon then, in that last agony of fear? Upon your good God, or little Angeline? Or upon the little Black Moustache?*

*Later on, they will reclaim you, bag of bones. And bury you with pomp and circumstance, and aged men will make orations. A little wooden cross will mark the spot and immortelles shall crown your chivalry, and Black Moustache will come and she will weep.*

On that one small promontory sixty thousand Frenchmen had been killed. The shrine they found, a virgin propped crookedly beside a trench whose side had sloughed in. She held in her arms a Bambino, and both Mother and Child had chipped noses, revealing the plaster beneath the tawdry colours.

*Piers said, "Queer, George, the hold religion has on men. Of all those dead fellows around us, I suppose each man called on God before he died."*
*"Some probably cursed Him," I suggested. "That boot I kicked – did you see? That poor beggar must have bowled right over, must have died with his*

*head in the mud. D'you think he called on his God. Piers? I doubt it."*

The battalion returned to the line filing into an old French trench. No lumber supports, no chicken-wire to hold up bulging walls of soggy soil, but great bundles of twigs and thin branches gathered thriftily hereabout. Pilk, the ingenious batman, had fashioned a mighty stick from one of them. It hung by a thong from the wrist. A stick for ratting. Rats were everywhere. Not apprehensive marauders ready to run at a sound. No. It is man who is on sufferance there. The line is the metropolis of the rodents, their Canaan, their happy hunting ground. It is their kingdom, reaching from the Channel to the Argonne. There never were such times, never such endless feasting! Yes, life goes easily with the rats. They have built this unseen realm underground, a honeycomb of runs, and each one leading to a grave. You may see their beaten tracks, and sometimes at night watch them migrate, moving shadows. Battalions of rats, brigades, divisions, whole army corps of them: silent, stealthy, wise. They slide over the parapet and flash back against the earth into their holes. They sit, beady eyed and insolent, returning stare for stare. Fat, oh monstrously fat, they are! Like cats, some of them. And others are diseased, with gaping ulcers on hairless flanks. But George learnt to use that big stick that hung always ready from his wrist. The stick that was his only weapon. Aim improving every day. He got tired of keeping count, so many rats beaten down into the slime, broken-backed, writhing.

The trench latrine was badly placed. The bucket sat crookedly in the mud in the recess that was too high. It was a humiliating ordeal, for it was necessary to crouch or take the risk of a sniper's bullet. An ordeal to be got through, somehow. Mud, chloride of lime, corruption. Decay, what is it, but a moment of matter's eternal commutations? Think of it like that. Be philosophic. In the open, in the privacy of the bush, the office of nature is without offence; an act of humility, an acknowledgement of the bond with Mother Earth. Soon decay will be cleansed, made sweet again. Manure. What fed the fruits of earth but corruption after all? And there a face, peering through the gap, beyond which the trench, regarding one's indignity stolidly, all unaware of it, seeing only a man in a latrine, and saying to him a necessary word. *"Keep your head down, sir; the snipers are busy this morning."*

A letter from home. Dorothy had moved from the seaside town to a Kentish village and tells George it is cheaper. The letter is a bare outline, but lying there in his bunk in the dim light of the deep dugout at Souchez Post, he built with his imagination a complete picture, detailed as a painted Dutch interior and just as vivid too. She tells him that Eric has made great friends with the smith. He is in and out of the forge all day. Her lodgings are nice and clean, the landlady is a decent women. But George worried, who will look out for this little woman with the two small children, a stranger drifted into the village? Hidden away in that Kentish village – shabby, poor, reserved and very proud; asking nothing, expecting nothing.

*The sector is no longer somnolent. The Saxons over there are becoming bellicose. Their evening hate no longer has the faint suggestion of apology; there is no prelude of warning fire high overhead, no facetious tattoo. Their machine guns open up viciously.*[x]

*Their artillery too, sprayed the Calonne sector, and the whine of shells was bitter on the air. And soon our own artillery replied, whiplashes upon the air; screaming, sinister and strangely exciting. The infantry watched the exchange. They had a secret contempt for all gunners. Making work for them, the endless futile work of trench repairs. Leave the Boche alone, and he would soon get tired.*

Rumours were on the air; the strafe presaged something. The long-expected attack on Vimy Ridge, perhaps, the shadowy battle that brooded over the sector week after week. Tunneling companies had been at it a long time, boring away beneath No Man's Land towards the flank of the scarred ridge. [In this prelude to the battle it was the far progress through these tunnels that so helped the Canadian advance on the ridge.] And perhaps counter-tunneling? Maybe thirty or forty feet beneath the Calonne Sector men were packing high explosives, piling them in that damp and earthy chamber; laying electric wires, mile long fuses. Well, one would never know. It would be a swift business, a pressing of a button somewhere over there. Finish.

George worried. He could not grasp what was expected of him as a platoon commander if there should be an attack. Not enough to resist.

---

[x] A possible indication that in spring 1917 the Germans knew that an attack on Vimy Ridge was imminent.

Orders would have to be given, a plan of action seen clearly through confusion, co-operation with one's flanks maintained. How could one impose one's will in confusion and turmoil? How would he make out when the great attack on Vimy came? Fear, there are so many shades of it. The shadowy forebodings of calamity that creep like fog, about the shrinking heart: that terror which topples and overthrows the citadel of the human soul. And between these two conditions all those anguishes whose discipline is the triumph of the soldier's soul and the measure of his quality. The man of imagination suffers most because he conjures up in his mind a thousand horrors that exist nowhere else, a thousand possibilities of evil. To him death comes not once, but many times. The stolid man meets danger when it comes with courage or without it. For him death calls but once. And each man has his own especial fear.

For George, shell fire, an ordeal was endurable: it did not penetrate to that last defence where, like a flame burning in still air, the soul abides apart. It left him master of his own essential self. But when the machine guns opened up the flame wavered, and fear blew icily through the chamber of ones soul. Shells were impersonal; machine gun fire searched for your entrails. Making them turn in your belly while your blood curdled. Under such fire he was no longer George, but one vast genital.

Once, coming back to headquarters along the communication trench under desultory shell fire the Colonel's batman was encountered coming out of H.Q. dugout. He carried a German helmet upside down, and cast its contents over the parapet. So the Colonel, it seemed, did not leave his dugout, even to relieve himself. Was the Colonel, then, a coward? No. Like his adjutant, who wore the ribands of the DSO and MC, he was a brave man. It seemed, then, that a man had so much physical courage and no more. Nerves, like the stoutest ropes, wore through, became tattered, thin and unreliable.

The battalion was out of the line. It had come out mud-coated and bedraggled. So now the men must find billets. To see every man fixed up, go over them all, and a word and a smile for each. Examine these damp wattle barns and consider the best arrangement of them, so that each man shall have the best accommodation possible and a chance of air. Seek out the source of each barn's water supply, walking the edge of the farmhouse dung-pile, considering seepage, filth. So many farmhouses, so many rectangular yards, so many dung-piles, walled round by wattle barns.

And then Pilk is at hand, faithful Pilk, dependable Pilk. "*A good billet, sir. Magnificent. Bit of luck I call it.*" A row of miners' tenements, looking bleakly towards a stark railway embankment spiked with signals: Rue St. Petersburgh.[x]

They were now some miles behind the front line. The rim of the ochreous tide of battle that eddied across the face of the land is a bitter memory, and no more. But the sound of the guns flows along its airy avenues and breaks in little

---

[x] This may have been in a tiny village such as Ham-en-Artois up against an embankment on the railway line from Lens through Bethune to Calais.

tremulous waves upon the ears. Now and again the windows oscillate and small objects become alive, with fast beating hearts. A homely sound at other times, but now, the recitative of death: maker of humble heart; remembrance of mortality. The guns.

Pilk explained the matter: he would draw rations for four and Madame would cook for them. And Madame would buy such extras as were needed, in short, do all the bartering, cooking, serving. And render an account weekly. And Madame smiled her understanding and agreement. She soon set before them such a meal as they had not tasted for many months. And to think she had made it out of bully beef. The coffee, in a great pot, was fragrant. They drank copiously, savouring the good taste of it. Madame, meanwhile had vanished to her own domain, a mysterious region barred by an immense cabinet. But a child remained, finger in mouth, wide-eyed and full of childish curiosity for strange men speaking words beyond her understanding.

*I beckoned the little thing, and she came, shyly, and sat upon my knee. I kissed her, fondled her flaxen hair. Was it her I kissed or my absent little son?* Godwin refers always to his son whereas this little girl might more probably have reminded him of his two year old daughter.

Watery winter wore on. The battalion returned to the line, rested, refreshed, re-equipped; yet without the buoyancy of fresh troops, without enthusiasm. They marched as men habituated to their lot and resigned to it all: hardship, hunger of heart, hunger of body, and the darkness wherein the future lay concealed from them, a menace and a hope. Why were these men there? For what were they fighting? If they were victorious, what would victory profit them? Victorious, they would return to their little homes, to their humble vocations, to their loves. And all would be as before. They would gain nothing, and less than nothing, for they would have lost, having given that which could not be returned to them, these years of their lives, Victory would grant them the residue of their days. Nothing more than that. And defeat? It would be the same. They would return; those who survived would cross the seas again, come back to their waiting farms, their little clearings, their young orchards. And all would be as before, save they would pay a little more here, a little more there, for tea, for tobacco, for daily bread. Victory, then, or defeat: it would be the same for them. They offered themselves, and they suffered all manner of evil, that all should be as it was with them.

Yet all changed. The wounded would carry their scars, the limbless go their ways upon stilts with metal members, grotesque and horrible, mocking their lovely limbs; the blind would grope their way about the world in darkness, asking of others news of the world they knew, hungering for the light. And the mad and the bereft, they would enter a merciful Elysium, the disordered realm of the insane. But the unwounded, the unscathed? They too would bear their scars, the scars of memory, the wounds upon the soul, unhealing, unhealable.

Why, then, were they there, upon that bleak road in northern France, marching in the soft, cold rain towards the line, towards the guns, towards another tour in the trenches?

Late autumn had merged into winter, and winter was now in turn upon its course towards spring. Not that there were as yet signs of the great stirring, for the lovely season tarried overlong, the skies continued grey, rain fell, day after day. So that it was seldom that the men knew the comfort of dry clothing, dry feet, or saw the face of the sun, warm and friendly, shining from a tattered sky.

George had now been six months in France. [Spring, 1917] A short time-period as men reckon it in the normal way of normal lives, with death away in some distant future so remote as not to merit a moment's uneasy thought. For then life appears as a freehold, a perpetuity. But here, where life was accepted gratefully in little nervous leases, from day to day, from week to week, aye, and now and then, from moment to moment, six months was not so much a span of days as a series of escapes from the outstretched hands of greedy death. Yes, six months in the line drew itself out, drew itself out interminably.

One day Piers announced that they were detailed for a bombing course. Temporary escape, it was true. Yet escape. Escape with honour. When they arrived they had been without sleep for more than forty hours. The excitement of the adventure had sustained George throughout the long tramp back. But now he suffered the reaction. Nature presented her account; he slumped upon his cot, inert, exhausted. His voice became husky, and presently the vocal chords failed entirely; he formed words but no sound came from his mouth. Moreover, he became wracked with cramp. And Pilk, solicitous, tended him, filling a wine bottle with hot water, placing it, thrust into a thick grey sock upon his belly. Having nothing to do there in the Nissen hut, a little later he began to occupy his time with the only literature at hand: manuals on bombing, treatises on high explosives. He read them contentedly in his cot. George reports that the M.O. looked in and, having examined him, asked how long he had been running a temperature. He said it would have been for weeks since many of the fellows carried on with a more or less consistent hundred or more and never knew it unless they cracked up. For six days George lay there and studied bombs and the actions of high explosives to while away the hours. Presently he became interested. On the seventh day, the last, the commandant set a written paper to his indifferent class. Still weak, but lacking other occupation, George passed the morning with pen and paper. Drawing the anatomy of bombs, British, French and German, was rather amusing.

The commandant had never seen such a paper, and said so. He shook his hand heartily. And so George received orders to report to the newly formed Divisional Training School. *

A week later he was in the tiny village of Lières, as an Instructor of the drafts that were to

---

* In letters written to Ted Roberts in British Columbia in the 1960s George refers to being sent off with Major Graham to form an instructional lot to give final training to men coming over from Canada. He remembers in the letter that he was only a subaltern but had the responsibility of an officer of field rank and wrote that he kept careful records and had trench maps and all sorts of minutiae.

come in next day for final intensive training before being drafted as reinforcements to battalions in the line. *

The Untrained Draft Company, now trained, was under orders to move up. Drab London buses clanked into the village and stood grotesquely there, unpainted, all their glory of red and white gone. How filthy to train men for battle and then stand and watch them go.

One day, while physical drill was in progress in the now-familiar orchard, George watched a clash between an instructor and a man in the ranks.

*"Put them arms up, put 'em right up!"* bawled the instructor. The man raised his arms shoulder high, but no higher. The instructor fumed. "Say, what's the idea? Can't you get an order"?

Something unpleasant was brewing. The order was repeated and now the squad was an audience watching a duel, keyed up, suppressed. Authority was challenged. The men stood, neutral, watching. Once again the offender raised his arms, shoulder high, but no higher. The time had come for action.

"Fall that man out!" I cried. A ripple of excitement passed over the ranks. The climax was at hand. "Now, what's the matter?" I asked.

He opened his grey shirt and bared a shoulder that was livid from the surgeon's knife and laced with the surgeon's stitches. So that's how it was, they were now shovelling the wounded back into the line; it was enough, it seemed if the man

---

* Lières is about one third of the way from Vimy to Calais and to this day a tiny village.

102

*could march. That would not do. I made a report. It lacked somewhat the coldness of official language and breathed my indignation. Presently I received orders to have the casualty ready to parade for medical inspection.*

*The M.O. came, asked a few indifferent questions, did no examination and pronounced him fit for service. The commandant merely shrugged. It was the Army.*

*I was furious. To send a man back into the line who could not handle a rifle; it was monstrous! Fit for service was he? Well, they would see.*

*So when the draft departed, their exit was watched by a ruddy-complexioned man from the field kitchens. The casualty was now on the strength of the Training School for rations and discipline. I chuckled. But he said nothing. And that was the Army too. It was known as a 'wangle'.*

*On the other side of the wall a young girl was playing upon a tinkling piano some jingle as paltry and infectious as Sur le Pont d'Avignon. Playing jingles on an ancient instrument in a meager little room to the counterpoint of the guns! Such a bombardment! Rising to a mad and maddening climax after a week's long crescendo, a climax that meant one thing: that the hour of the assault on the Ridge was at hand. How strange, to be there and alone, in this little room, with a girl playing jingles beyond a dividing wall, with the homely clack of hens from the yard below, and all the soft, murmurous sounds of village life on the soft air – somnolent, sweet – with the hour of battle at hand.*

*Such gunfire could not last indefinitely; this storm of death that drenched the trenches (and the men in those trenches, cowering, unnerved, fearful,*

103

*knowing the import of it must pass, must surely pass. This means the climax. Battle.* The adjuvant came and said: "We've taken the Ridge and they're consolidating the position." He spoke as though he himself had had a hand in it. The next day on the evening of the 10th of April George met the Major and asked if there was news of casualties, but there was nothing definite.* Reports filtered through and presently there was word that both Piers and Pilk had fallen. Nearly fifty years later on reading the history of the 29th Battalion sent to him by Ted Roberts, George wrote *"that he found the details of the action at Vimy in which a man dear to him was killed, and the details of his death he was never able to secure before the account given in the book."* He named the friend as Ben Gray, the man to whom he dedicated his novel *Why Stay We Here?.* George described the work as an account of the 29th at that stage of the war *"when everybody was properly brassed off with it".*

*It was leave at last, after nine months of it, and an extra clear twelve hours ahead of time. A wangled parade and expert lorry-hopping had done that. An extra day, or an extra night: either very precious. My spirits rose, and against the rhythmic music of the train I chanted to myself: and the wheels of the train beat time for me. So I sang, but not with my voice, for words came with a thick harshness that no amount of self-doctoring relieved. It was in my heart that I sang, thinking of England, of Dorothy, of the children.*

---

* The battle of Vimy Ridge lasted from April 7-14, 1917.

Dorothy asked: "What's wrong with your voice?" He didn't know, it had been like that for some time. They were at breakfast in the shabby little front room, with its melancholy lace curtains and patterned wallpaper, its plush chairs. Dorothy watched him closely and saw that he looked much older, his face was grey, his eyes pouched. And thin. How thin he was. A wreck, she thought. She insisted that he report sick. George reports he weighed only 118 pounds, 50 pounds less than usual. His temperature was a hundred and two. The M.O. said he would have to go to hospital and they would know the cause better after a bacteriological examination. But he didn't go to hospital. The bacteriological test was negative. He was passed fit for home service only.

Dorothy had found a cottage, a little workman's cottage that had passed through the hands of an artist. A hand pump supplied spring water and it was cold and sweet. Very sweet it tasted after the chlorinated water of France. He was able to come home sometimes on weekend leave thirty-seven miles away by bicycle.

Life in the Reserve Battalion went sluggishly through each day's routine. There was no enthusiasm in the ranks, nor any among the officers. There was the routine round; they did it conscientiously, but without any driving enthusiasm. Wangling had become an art, practiced with skill and cunning. Leave warrants were its prizes. He did what he was told to do, mechanically. He prosecuted without enthusiasm at district courts-martial. He defended men before them, acting as prisoner's friend, fighting obstinately for acquittals; getting them, with his rasping voice, his

105

face white and drawn, the ghost of the man he had been. Sometimes as he crossed the parade ground he felt it swaying gently under foot. At night he coughed, and there was a pain that shot, hot and cruel in the side. The men in the adjoining cubicles banged upon the thin partitions. He was keeping them awake, damn it.

At the cottage door the garden rustled in the November sun. Across the fields came the sound of bells from the village church. But this was not the customary peal, no. This was a mad peal, wild and free. Something odd about such bell-ringing. Armistice had been declared! He commanded that Dorothy come forth to hear the carillon from the village church. He was very excited and could not keep still. But Dorothy was at her ironing, and she returned to it until the last little garment had been pressed, and thereafter hung upon the line to air.

The Colonel sent for him and told him there was something mighty wrong with him and to report sick. This time the bacteriological report came back marked *positive.* George went into hospital.

*They put me to bed and at night a volunteer nurse from the V.A.D turned me about. She did it expertly. She spoke of pleurisy. There was a chart above my cot. The man in the next cot said he had tuberculosis same as me. I did not have tuberculosis. Oh, dear, no. I was there because of the pain in my side. Pleurisy. And because of the damnable cough, and my voice that went back on me. I determined to ask the M.O. But when he came, I remained mute in the presence of this famous physician, for all the Army had made of me nothing* but a captain. So it was the little V.A.D who told me the truth in the end but reproached me for she found it beastly to tell. She went away quickly. She was very young. I accepted the sentence with bitterness.

But the pleurisy cleared up and I was allowed to get up. I was boarded and marked for transport home but I had no wish to go. What about Dorothy and the children? Dorothy and the children would have to stay where they were. My pay would go on; I would be in hospital. I could assign the whole lot of it. Yes, that was true enough. There was nothing for it but to submit.

# Balfour Sanatorium

A fortnight later Godwin sailed out of Liverpool on a hospital ship bound for Portland, Maine. Nine days out, so that soon the ship, with its strange human freight, would make a landfall, would find Casco Bay and its multitude of islands somewhere along the dim arc of the horizon, and come to rest in Portland harbour. Bringing home the debris of the war, carrying home a little of the reality of it. For all the men Portland was the first glimpse of home, as it were. Soon they would be in Canada; meanwhile there was America, and the difference seemed small. For George each day widened the distance between himself and Dorothy and the children. It was exile for him. Dorothy and the children might have returned to Canada with him and in Whonnock perhaps have awaited his discharge from hospital. But there was no money to bring them there, no money at all.

At Liverpool there had been no demonstration. The men merely embarked, and that was all. True, in each cabin there was a letter in the hand of the King, thanking them, wishing them God-speed; but beyond that courtesy there was nothing.

But how hearty the welcome in Portland. They filed to the waiting train, or were carried to it, and it was white and very beautiful. Beside each cot were gifts: books, fruit, chocolate, cigarettes, everything a man might care about with a journey ahead of him. George arrived in Vancouver six days later. The air had tinged his face with bronze and he was lean, he looked a healthy man.

It would be a year's job, they told him at the hospital, before he was right. He must go up into the mountains, give the lung tissue time to heal. Then he would be as well as before. Well, nearly as well: an arrested case. His orders were to take the train into the interior of British Columbia, to the Balfour Military Sanatorium on the hills by Kootenay Lake where the mountain air would cure him.

The Sanatorium was converted from a hotel that had been opened only a few years earlier and was magnificently situated just above the Ferry Landing in Balfour at the entrance to the west arm of Kootenay Lake. After the six day train journey from Portland Maine via Montreal, Toronto, the Prairies and the Rocky Mountains to Vancouver they entrained again for the winding railroad through Southern British Columbia via Hope and then, as part of the Kettle Valley Railway, through the Coquihalla Valley to Penticton, Midway and Nelson where they disembarked. The last part of the journey was by one of the lake steamers twenty miles to Balfour.

The building was three and a half stories in height. Two sides of the ground floor had a wide covered veranda previously open to the air, but now glassed in for protection from winter cold, without obscuring views of the lake. At one end a roofed but open tower had been created to enhance the enjoyment of the scenery. A large rotunda on the ground floor with a fine stone fireplace designed originally for fine occasions in the hotel had been preserved. On the second floor many of the bedrooms were joined together into single wards with beds for twelve. In his room

George had two photographs of Eric and Monica. He remembered that there were a hundred or so of us in care. At the rear of the building there was an annexe for nursing staff and storage and recreational therapy. Therapy was varied and active. They wove baskets and trays furiously and gave them as prizes to local youngsters. The grounds were sloped and cleared with wide paths on which they could walk at leisure. There were tennis courts for those who wished. Behind this grand building the hills were partially treed and rose to the Kokanee Mountains and the Kokanee Glacier.

In the summer there were pleasant strolls among the nearby orchards on the south facing slopes and, in the winter, walks in the brisk air and lightly snow covered hills. It was hard to be nostalgic for Europe in these lovely surroundings.

George spent a year through the summer and winter of 1918-1919 at the 'san' and it was there he later claimed he had fallen in love with a sweet occupational therapist who he felt sure would have reciprocated that love had she not been the daughter of a strict Presbyterian family. An upbringing and moral certitude that would not allow her to become involved with a married man the father of two young children. It was twenty years later at the time of the Second World War that they met again and entered into correspondence that will be referred to later.

At the end of the year at Balfour George was returned to England, to home and family. Family life was reinstated with their first family home in Kensington where the second son Geoffrey was born in 1921. William was born three years later followed by the last child Tony in 1926. In 1929 the family moved to Shoreham on the Sussex coast to a large Victorian house set in an established orchard of apples, pears and plums, the whole enclosed by a high flint wall. Of the two elder children, Monica attended the *Lycée Française* in South Kensington and Eric completed his time at St Paul's School before entering St Mary's Medical School in Edinburgh.

# A career in writing

The two books considered so far, his most significant though neither fully appreciated at the time, were brought to light when republished in the 1990s. They were written some years after Godwin's homestead and war experiences and brought out his inner feelings of the stupidity of war. Godwin chose the title for the book *Why Stay We Here?* from Christopher Marlowe's *Dido*.

> *The Grecian soldiers, tired with ten years' of war,*
> *Began to cry: "Let us unto our ships;*
> *Troy is invincible: why stay we here?"*

He wrote with feeling about his colleagues, both junior and senior to him. He addressed their fears and beliefs, their bravery, injuries and deaths. He took a philosophical view of war, the relentless machine that is the army and the turmoil that those with religious faith met in the face of such terrible waste of life. *Why Stay we Here?* was published in 1930 by Philip Allan & Co. Ltd. in London. A year before the same publisher had released *The Eternal Forest Under Western Skies* which Godwin dedicated to his wife. In 1948 he donated a signed copy of this book to the University of British Columbia for inclusion in the Howay-Reid Collection of books dealing with Canadian History.

Just before penning these two books and still affected by his trials in Whonnock, Godwin wrote a small commentary on what he saw as a possible future for North America. It was titled *Columbia, or the Future of Canada* (Kegan 1928).

He wrote that Canada's future would ultimately be decided by her people. The majority of those people in fifty years, with the exception of an all-French Quebec and a threatened all-Asian British Columbia, would be of mixed cosmopolitan descent he predicted. He also wrote that sooner or later, and almost certainly inevitably, Canada would be joined as one with the United States of America. By absorption Canada would lose her Imperial Preference and gain the vast markets of the United States and participation in the steadily increasing South American trade. Taxation would decrease and railway development between the two united halves of the Continent would facilitate movements of population and produce. The present sea-route via Montreal and the St. Lawrence, closed for months of the year, would be replaced by the shorter and more logical Great Lakes – New York route, open the year round. Her Provinces, transformed into self-governing States would remain autonomous. The present top-heavy system of government, with its hordes of salaried, non-producing drones, would disappear. To-day, he wrote, these numerous law-makers house themselves magnificently amidst the poverty of those for whom they legislate; while the Senate is nothing but the sanctuary of the guardian angels of the vested interests, among whom you may look in vain for a single horny hand. The anachronism of a series of petty, semi-regal courts such as now support the dignity of Governor General and Lieutenant Governors, with the inevitable concomitants of snobbery and shameless extravagant expenditure would disappear. The reader will recognize where he was right and where he was not.

In the late 1920s Godwin worked on a biography of Captain George Vancouver, *Vancouver a Life*. Much of Vancouver's life had been hidden or forgotten until the early part of the twentieth century. Professor Edmund Meany of Washington University did much to revive the memory of Vancouver and published an annotated edition of that part of the *Voyage of Discovery* which deals with the exploration of Puget Sound. In 1923, GH Anderson of King's Lynn wrote a brief but very valuable monograph on the Vancouver family's association with that town. Judge Howay of New Westminster, CF Newcombe of Vancouver and LV Denton and John Housie of the British Columbian Historical Association went in search of new material.

Godwin was able to unearth a large number of hitherto overlooked Vancouver dispatches, letters and charts together with a number of notes upon persons and subjects of historical interest. Searching of the archives which resulted in the discovery of this new material was carried out by Mrs Violet Heddon, to whom Godwin expressed his thanks and gratitude. Often the deciphering of the faded ink proved to be no easy matter, and there were bundles of manuscript whose identification called for patience, knowledge and enthusiasm. Thanks to the help and support of many others he was able to have Appleton and Company of New York publish the book (*Vancouver a Life*. D Appleton and Company. New York. 1931). Publication was achieved after he was unable to interest any Canadian publishers. The first part of the book related the life and travels of the man, the second, a lengthy appendix, included much of the unearthed information referred to and the letters of Vancouver from 1790 to 1798.

Some of Godwin's thoughts on Vancouver's seminal achievements in those harsh years of the late eighteenth century are reproduced here.

*Given command of the Nootka Expedition in December 1790 was the turning point in Vancouver's career. It was his great opportunity and he took it. During the next four years he was to make discoveries that stand out in a century of great voyages of discovery and place its commander among the greatest of eighteenth-century explorers.*

In Godwin's research of the Discovery's voyage it became obvious that, mobility, elaborate modern scientific equipment and easy communications with the outside world had robbed exploration of much of its rigours. It was well to conjure up as best as possible the condition under which these great voyages of the pre-steam, pre-radio age worked. Such an enterprise was warranted to find the fundamentally big qualities of a man such as Vancouver, as it was certain to unmask latent weaknesses. Cooped up in that small ship, the men in their ill-lit and malodorous forecastle quarters frequently fell to quarrelling. Enforced propinquity is a certain breeder of animosities that grow in time to deep and brooding hate. Vancouver punished the men who quarreled and fought by giving them the lash. But the psychological drama of the forecastle was not peculiar to that part of the ship's company. The commander had to keep the upper hand of his crew and to suppress brawling. He had to handle mettlesome "young gentlemen" of the quarter-deck and teach them by the rough methods of his time the meaning of sea discipline. He did not hesitate to prescribe the same medicine for the peer's son as for the son of the farmer and labourer. He had to preserve harmony among his officers and, between them and himself, maintain mutual respect and loyalty.

In short, in those days a commander had but two alternatives: to be the autocratic ruler of an isolated floating society, or to expose himself to ignominious death at the hands of a mutinous crew. Vancouver new this as well as any man afloat.

In Godwin's examination of Vancouver's great achievements and of his Great Chart he was impressed with how he honoured his officers, all of whose names are to be found perpetuated in geographic features along the coast and how he remembered friends and relatives and the place-names of his native country. His attitude was that of a scientific man: he sought everywhere proof, and, whenever possible, even when so ill that with difficulty he could drag himself about, went in person in the ship's yawl upon long and arduous expeditions. Even so, in the making of the Great Chart, an achievement that gives him a place of permanent importance in the history of discovery, he failed to detect two of the greatest rivers on the Pacific coast. In later years these failures brought his reputation for sagacity into question. His first failure was the missing of the great Columbia River.

On April 27, 1792, he wrote, "*On the south side of the promontory was the appearance of an inlet, or small river, the land behind not indicating it to be of any great extent."* He next notes significant changes in the water. *"The sea has now changed from its natural, to river coloured water; the probable consequence of some streams falling into the bay."*

Why did Vancouver on this occasion fail to read fairly obvious river signs? Godwin considered that the only theory that seemed to meet this extraordinary failure in such a navigator is that Vancouver had approached the examination of this coast with a bias against the possibility of the existence of great navigable waterways. In any case having gazed upon the estuary of the great Columbia River, he proceeded north without suspecting its existence.

Vancouver's next failure was of equal interest, since he was himself in the yawl that made the particular expedition that should have led to the discovery of the great Fraser River. It is true that he had plenty of evidence from which he might have deduced the existence of a large river; but it must be borne in mind that the Fraser does not terminate in a wide, easily seen, open estuary, but in a delta. In passing Point Roberts Vancouver could have seen the bluff that he named Point Grey in the distance. As he made his way along the coast Vancouver wrote *"The coast presented a task of examination to which we conceived our equipment very unequal."* But if he missed the Fraser River, he did not return to the *Discovery* with nothing accomplished. Sailing northwards around Point Grey he came through the narrow opening and entered the inlet he named Burrard's Channel. As he left the next day through that narrow opening he wrote; *"the land upon the southern shore*

117

*presented an unbroken line of standing timber, silent and inscrutable; while to the north, the hump of a mountain raised itself against the skyline."* If he missed two rivers he missed little else.

Vancouver had been ordered to Nootka *"to receive back, in form, a restitution of the territories on which the Spaniards had seized and also to make an accurate survey of the coast, from the 30th degree of north latitude north-westward".* When Spain had agreed by the "Nootka Convention" to restore the disputed territory to Great Britain, Don Juan Francisco de la Bodega y Quadra, commander-in-chief of the marine establishment of St Blas and California, was ordered north to hand over in form. Like Vancouver, Quadra had his orders; like Vancouver he put his own interpretation upon them. The orders were not clear and the pair could not agree to the bounds of the territory to be formally ceded by one to the other. Godwin suggested that either man might have been forgiven had he allowed an element of acrimony to enter into the negotiations. To their eternal honour, both parties behaved like the gentlemen they were.

Arising from his voyages, Vancouver's appreciation of the vast potentialities of the Pacific at a time when the world knew little of it, and cared less, when the only people to penetrate there besides the Spanish were fur-traders in search of sea-otter, is really extraordinary. He analysed the potential dangers of the Spanish policy of secrecy; noted the character of that people and put his finger upon the essential weakness of their administration. He realized that this country the Spaniards called New California, with its vast seaboard and rich and fertile hinterland, must one

118

day become thickly peopled by a race virile enough to hold and develop it. He undoubtedly foresaw the dispossession of the Spanish, who sat in that fat land with nothing but a skeleton garrison to guard their new Canaan.

Vancouver's voyages to Owhyhee in the Sandwich Islands (Hawaii), so fertile and beautiful, set in mid-Pacific, convinced Vancouver that here was a prize worth securing for the British crown. Not by force of arms but by cession. The argument that Vancouver advanced to King Tamaahmaah, leaving him to debate the matter in private with the chiefs, was that of protection. It was a cogent argument, namely, that King George could and would protect the islands from the molestations of passing ships. On February 25, 1794, Tamaahmaah and the principal chiefs of the island, after due consideration, unanimously ceded the island of Owhyhee to his Britannic Majesty, and acknowledged themselves to be subjects of Great Britain. However, Vancouver's prize was never gained. The islands though undoubtedly ceded, were never a British possession, since the cession was never confirmed by the Government, then far too preoccupied with affairs in Europe to concern itself with obscure islands in mid-Pacific.

Godwin writes that the original manuscript of Vancouver's lengthy record of his five adventurous and fruitful years of exploration had been lost. A page found in the unindexed documents of the British Museum showed that not only was Vancouver actually the author of the works signed by him, but also how he wrote, and how he dealt with the revision of his manuscript before such time as weakness involved his brother in that task. Unfortunately, after publication of the first edition of his *Voyage of Discovery* with the atlas, the copper plates of the charts were all stolen. When it is remembered that Vancouver was at sea when most boys are at school, that his whole life, until the end of his great voyage, was spent afloat, then this written record of his activities, his own composition, becomes a most impressive performance. By modern day standards, as Godwin considered it, his *Voyage of Discovery* is over long and the writing somewhat prosy, yet by some magic or other the reader is at last won to its author. His character, as it were, keeps breaking through the stilted conventional style. He is modest, generous in tributes to his officers and to the navigators of other nations, whose work he tests carefully and then shrewdly judges. He is meticulous in regard to all facts, judicial and scientifically cautious. Godwin sensed the iron will of the man and the indomitable courage that never contemplated defeat; and there was something fine and rugged in this spirit housed in a frail and failing body so close to his death at the age of forty-one.

Godwin's novel, *The Mystery of Anna Berger* was first published in 1935 and made part of the "Thinker's Library" in 1948. It was written as his response to try and learn more about the disease that by coincidence later threatened his granddaughter's life. The book told of a young girl in a remote Tyrolean village who became absorbed with a love of Christ. She eat little or nothing, except that of the daily sacrament offered by the local Priest, developed the stigmatic wounds of Christ on the cross and experienced periodic episodes of holy ecstasy. Godwin reveled in writing about the differences of belief and attitude between the local parish priest, steeped in catholic reverence, and the Jewish doctor, determined to find a medical explanation, who was asked to attend her. Anna, a centre of Catholic veneration, and her family, the local priest and the little remote village, became an attraction to people from wide and near bringing wealth into the community. As her passion and hysteria worsened she progressively became more physically ill and died. Although George's story was not based on that single life he took the opportunity to research and mention many similar examples expounded by the Catholic Church. Some of these events had been accepted by the church as factual, but others were not confirmed. His own views on the subject were not hidden from the reader!

Once back in England, and through the later nineteen twenties and thirties, Godwin was fairly successful writing books and doing freelance and, without making a fortune, earned enough for a high standard of living, the fulfillment of educational aspirations for his children and an annual trip abroad. He wrote the biography of George Vancouver, *The Eternal Forest* and *Why Stay we Here?* discussed in detail already. He also wrote *Cain, or the future of Crime* and *Columbia or the Future of Canada*, both published by Kegan, Paul, Trench, Trubner & Co. in London in 1928. In the early thirties he penned *Discovery (The story of the Finding of the World)* (1933) and a futuristic novel, *Empty Victory* (1932). In 1936 he published a three act play *The Disciple* based on the lives of apprentices in Milan at the time of Leonardo da Vinci.

At the outset of the Second World War Godwin was working for Acorn Press in Curzon Street. He was on the Officer Emergency Reserve and fully expected to be in the army again soon. He didn't mind since the action of the state had deprived him of a living. He felt that he might as well become an insignificant part of the war machine. However, it didn't come to that because he was turned down. He had not done much writing of his own for some time. A small commissioned book had just been finished, *The Land of the Larder* (1939), the story of the Surfleet Experiment and its significance in war. The experiment took place on a farm near Surfleet in Lincolnshire and lasted just two years from 1935. It involved the use of humus made using the '*Indore Process*' developed by Sir Albert Howard during his time in India. The conversion of animal and vegetable waste into humus was said to improve the health and quality of crops and livestock. Godwin had also published an official history of Queen Mary College of London University (1944). He thought he made a very nice book of it. One thousand five hundred copies had just been bound when the war came.

During the war Godwin became involved in various propaganda writing for the Government. As this became more and more boring he lightened things by writing a small pamphlet on faith healing, *Priest or Physician,* published by Watts and Company in 1941. To keep himself occupied, and in time for the two hundredth anniversary of the Samuel Hanson and Sons Company, he wrote and had privately printed *Hansons of Eastcheap 1747-1947.* The book was really an excuse to research and write about the history of the import and export of various foodstuffs, including spices, fruits, tea, coffee, groceries and even wine. The title of the book indicated it was about Samuel Hanson and the grocery business he opened in 1747 in Botolph Lane, later incorporated in the widening of Eastcheap, and its development and expansion over the next two hundred years. George took the opportunity to also write about the import of a wide variety of food stuffs extending back to early Christian times. He wrote of the changes the transition from the non-mechanical to the age of machines had made. Further the way the gathering speed of the advance of science and discovery had had direct effects upon the grocer and his trade. Not least where the new science applied itself to the preservation of foods and to the analysis of their purity. He commentated on the influence members of the grocery trade had on the political scene in London. Sir Reginald Hanson was one of 39 grocers who served as Lord Mayor of London over the centuries.

# Law and Family

At the end of his year at Balfour George was returned to England, to home and family. Family life was reinstated with their first family home in Kensington where the second son Geoffrey was born in 1921. William was born three years later followed by the last child Tony in 1926. In 1929 the family moved to Shoreham on the Sussex coast to a large Victorian house set in an established orchard of apples, pears and plums, the whole enclosed by a high flint wall.

Godwin wrote little about his wife but did leave thoughts of his children in letters to Dr Ethlyn Trapp and in the record of his son Geoffrey's transatlantic sail.

Eric, his first child, was born in the homestead in British Columbia in 1913 and was the apple of his eye and the one he missed most dreadfully in France. Why then did they have problems? He wrote in one of his letters that father son difficulty was hard to analyse and understand. The root of George's bitterness was buried in rejected deep love and devotion. That sort of wound hurt and continued to hurt all ones days. What George felt he should have done was suspend judgment. Eric continued a source of grief to him. They seldom saw each other. In 1939 Eric was involved in a terrible accident in which his oldest school friend was killed when Eric was driving. George stood by Eric and went to the inquest with him. Only afterwards did he learn that he had been given an entirely lying account of the accident and so added by repeating it under oath, perjury to what was mighty near manslaughter. Geoffrey, with characteristic generosity, excused him, but this ghastly tragedy was just one more in a long chain of things Eric did to grieve and hurt. *"Why should the son upon whom one perhaps so unjustly, spent what should have been spread over them all, repay one like that? "*

At the outset of the war Eric joined the Royal Army Medical Corps (RAMC). Dorothy's cousin was the General commanding the RAMC and they had thought that if Eric did well he might keep a friendly eye on him. Eric was married some months before Dunkirk and took part in the retreat. He described his involvement in a letter he sent. *"We went over to assist in treating the wounded who were being brought to the quay at Dunkirk. They were lying among big bales of wool scattered about, which gave quite good protection. When the hospital ships came in we loaded them on the run with showers of shrapnel bombs falling round us. It was loaded up and away in half an hour".*

Eric completed his time at St Paul's School before entering St Mary's Medical School in Edinburgh. He became a consultant anaesthetist to a group of hospitals in Croydon.

Monica was born in Belfast on January 21, 1916, not in British Columbia as Godwin had suggested in the *Eternal Forest*. Monica attended the *Lycée Française* in South Kensington and became a graduate of the Sorbonne. She taught school, worked for a time at the Foreign Office and took a PhD at Newnham College, Cambridge. She was Senior French Mistress at the Leys School a large school in Cambridge.

Monica's second child, Suzanna, a pretty and charming little girl got it into her head that she was getting fat and began to abstain from food, covering up her uneaten meals one way and another. She fell away and became a tragic little figure and in need of medical and psychological help. George new something of the situation because some years before he became fascinated with the subject. The result was a novel *The Mystery of Anna Berger* in which he wrote about an Austrian girl who starved herself and exhibited the wounds of Christ. It was a morbid subject, but George felt he would like to understand the emotional mechanisms of it. He was able to suggest to Monica that Suzanna might be the victim of globus hysterica or anorexia nervosa as it came to be known. Monica passed on the information to her G.P. who sent her to the Neurological Hospital in London. After several weeks in hospital and fear of death, which she was told would result if she refused food, acted to brace her to put up a fight. As she ate, so she regained weight and became less like an emaciated wreck. While the ordeal lasted it put a strain on everyone especially on Monica who motored 30 miles a day each way to see the child and stay the three hours permitted to ward off the ever flowing tears that followed every demand denied. Suzanna's elder sister, Lucy, remembers the situation differently and wrote passionately about her sister's fall into drugs and degradation leading ultimately to an early death.

Sometimes, George wrote, he would sit in his office - which for him was far nicer than many a sitting room – and ponder Geoffrey (1921-1967). He would never work at school. Three times he ran away and three times George had a job to find him and get him back. He went to sea as a deck boy, crossing the Atlantic in winter, and up to the Arctic on a trawler. For a year he worked as a deck hand on a seagoing yacht. He was the problem son. He gave his father sleepless nights; George agonized when he thought he watched the life flutter from his lips with pneumonia and measles. He agonized when he fenced with the police to get him out of some scrape or other. At the age of thirteen Geoffrey tried to steal an airplane to fly it to kill Mussolini!

Yet so ignorant and lazy, he could write like an angel and wrote and published short stories that anyone might be proud to have written. There are more avenues than books, other criteria than diplomas and degrees. At eighteen Geoffrey joined the RAF insisting on doing so two years before his time. He loved the water and was in the motorboat section of coastal command. He then started to have things published in Penguin Parade and others and the BBC dramatized one of his stories for a broadcast play.

In 1966 Geoffrey single handedly crossed the Atlantic in a tiny sloop with fiberglass hull and marine ply superstructure named after his wife, *Penny Ballerina.* The crossing was successful but a year later sailing with a British Columbian Cree-Indian, Larry Rodney, the yacht and crew were lost without trace.

William Henry (b.1923), Billy, was the bright one. He had attended St Paul's Preparatory School prior to the Lycée Francais de Londres. He won himself an Open State Scholarship, valued £100 a year for three years, and entered St John's College Cambridge. He did well and obtained a 2.2 BA in English in 1945 and was awarded MA in 1948. He was particularly fond of his Tutor CW Guillebaud, the famous economist who wrote extensively on the subject (including the economics of the Nazi regime) and undertook reviews of the National Health Service. William went on to do well and as Assistant Treasury Solicitor he acted as Agent for the United Kingdom of Great Britain and Northern Ireland versus the Commission of the European Communities in a dispute on subsidies for pig farmers.

Tony (b.1926) was the youngest and reacted rather strangely to that position. Being smallest and weakest he got feelings of inadequacy compared to his elder brothers. His attitude to life was a defensive one. He was tall with a Grecian appearance. George felt that he knew him better than the others and were very united. His trouble had been in part a reaction to his mother's inability to give him demonstrative love and much of his naughtiness in his younger years came from that and was a form of punishing her. As a teenager he had developed almost complete self-control, though it cost him much to learn it. When Dorothy and the children left London for Cambridge at the beginning of the war Tony went to Perse School a leading school founded in 1615. He became a most successful lawyer and senior partner in a major firm in Singapore.

In the late 1930s George met again with Ethlyn Trapp, the woman who had looked after him in the sanatorium in Balfour. She had become a physician specializing in radiation treatment of cancer. Godwin had seen her signature in the visitor's book of the Radiumhemmet in Stockholm when he visited on one of his annual trips to Europe a year or two before. Why he had chosen to visit a cancer hospital in Sweden is not known, though perhaps just an example of his extraordinary diversity of interests. Perhaps it was just another search for a subject of interest that he might choose to write about. When Dr Trapp was in England, undertaking post graduate studies in Manchester at the Christie Hospital and Holt Radium Institute, she had been to London and they had met for lunch and strolled together on the Temple Lawn which he described as at its greenest. But at lunch they were not in rapport. The magic of the British Columbian scenery and the closeness of caregiver and patient were not to be repeated. However, during the early part of the Second World War they entered into correspondence. In a series of letters he told her of the happenings in London and his affection for her. Any letters of hers to Godwin, which were presumably sent in response, are not available. Following the bombing of the Temple buildings and his injuries the letters fell away and were not resumed until 1970. Godwin sent Dr Trapp a copy of Geoffrey's log of his Atlantic voyages and she told him of her meeting in Vancouver with Monica and Tony. They shared mutual regrets at aging and opportunities lost.

In the year previous to the War his legal fees had risen to nearly £2,000 by dint of hard work, but when war broke out his income dried up almost completely. The family had to leave their London Home. The Lycee Francaise where Bill and Tony went was evacuated to Cambridge. Dorothy and the boys were in a little villa there which became their new home. George went at weekends but otherwise stayed in Curzon Street where he slept on a lilo on the floor. He took his tiny wireless and put it by his side to listen to the news bulletins and the English traitor's nightly tirades from a German wireless station. Only later did they find out that this was William Joyce, nicknamed Lord Haw-Haw for his nasal voice caused in one of many fights he had had as a young man. He broadcast throughout the war. Joyce was captured just before the end of hostilities in Hamburg and hanged as a traitor on January 3,1946.

George opined that there was nothing 1914-ish about this war. Man was beginning to be afraid of his own wickedness. There was such a shocking discrepancy between the instruments of slaughter he had invented out of the wickedness of his heart and his own defenceless, soft and vulnerable flesh and blood body.

With the German capture of Norway in April, 1940 the supply of paper dried up almost completely. As with many other writing men George was in the position of a carpenter who knew his job but could get no wood to work on. His normal source of revenue, the newspapers and magazines and publicity people dried up entirely. He had to move from Curzon Street and close down his little publishing efforts, though as a defiant end to it he continued in publishing a small book on woodlands. His new abode was a jolly little place he was fortunate enough to snap up for a very low rent at 2, Harcourt Building in the Temple. He had two rooms and slept in the smaller. He continued to go home at weekends and furiously tried to grow food in their tiny garden.

Early in 1940 the Government started schemes to evacuate children from London and other major cities to live in the countryside where there would be less danger from German bombs. They also encouraged children to be sent to Canada or Australia. By the summer over 1,000 children had arrived safely in Canada. Dorothy and George felt that their youngest, Tony, should be offered the opportunity to escape the risks and they were both thrilled that Ethlyn Trapp, the wonderful therapist whom George had so admired at the Sanatorium in Canada after the First World War, and now a respected physician in Vancouver, had offered to take the boy. The scheme was made available for children of grant-aided schools such as Perse School in Cambridge where Tony was a pupil making him eligible for transport. They accordingly filled in all the forms and had him medically examined. He was passed and then all they had to do was wait. But then there were doubts, the scheme was suspended for a while then reinstated. But the scheme was abandoned forever with the ghastly sinking of one of the ships. The *City of Benares* was torpedoed on September 17, 1940, at dead of night in fierce seas 600 miles at sea. There were 406 people aboard ninety of whom were children and only thirteen of the little ones survived. A terrible act that left George unchanged in his mind about the Hun, and he swore he was through with Germans forever! The *City of Benares* had been built as a luxury liner on the Clyde in 1936 and was named after the holy city on the Ganges. Prime Minister Churchill ordered a stop to the evacuation of British children to Canada on

September 23, two days before the last of the survivors were rescued.

At about the same time George was offered two jobs after nearly a year of only odd jobs. He was involved in producing propaganda material for the war effort. A companion book to *The Land our Larder*, also published by Acorn, finally came out, though it had been held up for a long time because he could not get a paper permit! He had written it to keep himself from going dotty when he had so few commissions. It concerned trees and was titled *Our Woods in War* (London, Acorn, 1940).

Late in 1940 the bombing of London came close to home with several land mines damaging parts of the Temple. The worst came on the evening of the first day of the New Year. Godwin described the events that followed in one of his letters to Dr Trapp. As he stood in his pygamas warming himself before the gas fire preparatory to going to bed, a land mine descended on the next house and wrecked his own place and catapulted him into a glass-panelled door. His nose was all but completely guillotined. It required fourteen stitches and two operations to put it back together. He suffered black eyes, a split mouth and a jaw so sore that he could not eat for days. He was away from the office for six weeks and had to move into the Savage Club at Carlton House Terrace. When his place was wrecked he sent daughter Monica to salve things, but within twenty-four hours looters had got in and taken three things; his gold watch, cash in a little tin box and the precious tea that Ethlyn had sent him from Canada in a Christmas care parcel. He was almost as wild about the tea as about the watch as its quality was a reminder of what tea had been like two years before.

Although Godwin had been called to the Bar in 1917 during the time he had been invalided back from France, he spent most of his time writing, both books and commissions and very little time in Law. There are two editions of the Law Register and two different addresses given - "50 Elsham Road, Kensington W.14 and 3 Plowden Buildings, Temple, E.C." However, he is recorded as a member of the South Eastern Circuit. In the 1950s he worked from 20, Old Buildings, Lincoln's Inn WC2.

Written in 1954 to coincide with the almost complete restoration of the Temple buildings after the devastating bombing of World War Two, Godwin published *The Middle Temple* a history of the Society and fellowship. The origin of the Society was to be found in The Knights Templars. The Order of the Knights Templars created in 1118 had as its purpose the organization of the dedicated knights and their people who defended the crusaders and the holy city of Jerusalem recovered for Christianity from the Saracens. The Order rapidly increased in numerical strength and in power derived from extraordinary privilege. In London they settled on the south side of Holborn, in the parish of St Andrew, and there they built a round church in the style of the Church of the Holy Sepulchre in Jerusalem. So high became the repute of the Templars that by the time of Henry II it was customary for the King's taxes to be placed with the Prior in the New Temple treasury for safe keeping. In time the Order came to play a prominent role in Court and national life and affairs. In these matters the Knights Templars had much routine business that called for the services of men learned in the law. A final decree against the Templars in England was made in 1312. After that date the Temple beside the Thames was no longer the home of the most colourful, the most noble, the most powerful of the great military Orders and the Age of Chivalry was dead. The Temple in time became the province of the lawyers. They became aligned with four separate Inns of Court and then into two main bodies the Middle Temple and the Inner Temple.

The Middle Temple escaped the fury of the Great Fire of London but was not so fortunate twelve years later. On the night of January 26, 1678, there was a hard frost and the fringes of the Thames were frozen. A small fire started in the Middle Temple where many of the buildings had not a single brick in their fabric, but only plaster and wood. The flames spread quickly, but no water could be drawn from the frozen Thames. As there was a small brewery on the west side of the Inner Temple Hall beer was pumped on to the flames and with the aid of gunpowder to demolish burning buildings the fire was confined, though with extensive damage to the Middle Temple. Five years later the brewery received £20 in compensation: "*In full satisfaction of Ale and Beere lost in the Fire which happened in the year 1678*".

Over the years the Middle Temple had many famous fellows, not all of whom were lawyers, including Sir Francis Drake, Oliver Goldsmith, Dr Johnson, Sir Martin Frobisher, Thackeray and Dickens. In addition it is worthy of note that five Middle Templars were signatories of the American Declaration of Independence, Edward Rutledge,

Thomas Heywood, Thomas Lynch, Thomas McKean and Arthur Middleton.

Godwin spent a few months in Chambers as a very junior resident before his move to British Columbia and his marriage. He was a very youthful student with no experience of housekeeping. So when an old woman presented herself at the door and offered to 'do' for him, he accepted her offer gratefully. She explained how she did for those before him and that everybody in the Temple knew Mrs Boddy. With that introduction, Mrs Boddy stepped across the threshold and took over her undefined – and as time was to prove – undefinable duties.

The terrible bombing of 1940, which badly damaged his chambers, wrought extensive damage to much of the Middle Temple and continued until the Battle of London was finally won. Destroyed, or badly damaged, were the Temple Church, the Master's House, the Cloisters, the Hall and Library, and one hundred and twelve sets of chambers of a total of two hundred and eighty-five sets. Until the end of the war nothing could be done but 'make – do and mend', with the sole object of securing dangerous structures, making roofs weather proof, and contriving as much accommodation as possible for those still living or working in the Inn. It was not until 1950, when building restrictions were lifted, that the real work of restoration could begin. As Godwin wrote in 1953-1954 the rebuilding of the Temple was proceeding apace. Wars, rebellions and the catastrophe of fires had tempered but not destroyed the beauty of that ancient place.

As the years rolled by Godwin wrote less, in part because he had suffered some brain damage in the bomb assault on his room at his Temple dwelling in the war. He also experienced difficulty in lucid speech which affected his ability to practice Law. It took time for him to relearn speech and even how to read. The last books he published were in 1956 and 1957. They both had to do with crime, *Crime and Social Action* and *Criminal Man.*

Godwin's interest in writing about crime began much earlier in 1937. He had been asked to pen an introduction to the English version of Professor Karl Berg's *Der Sadist* (The Library of Abnormal Psychological Types). The book dealt with the crimes of Peter Kürten in the early 1900s. His intended introduction became too long for its original purpose and it was therefore turned into a small book rather than be part of a large one. In the thirty years leading up to his final arrest Peter Kürten had spent more than 20 years in prison for a litany of sadistic crimes including many attempted strangulations, attacks with daggers and knives, innumerable arsons and several murders. The murders involved one man and several women and children all involving sexual gratification. Most were carried out when living in Düsseldorf in the sixteen months leading to his final arrest that created a Reign of Terror in that city. In the ten months from arrest to execution Kürten's background and psychology were studied intensively. Professor Berg concluded that he presented no aspect of psychopathology but did raise in an unmistakable way urgent problems in penology. It was not possible to study this product of bad heredity, plus more than twenty years of prison life, without pondering the effect of prison in changing a pervert and psychopath into an arch criminal and an enemy of his kind. Kürten remained impassive to the end. He confessed that when Professor Berg's woman doctor assistant entered his cell the desire to strangle her was almost irresistible. And when he knew he was to die at the hands of the executioner on the following morning, he asked, almost eagerly: "Shall I hear the gush of my own blood? That would be the pleasure of pleasures!"

Twenty years after *Der Sadist* Godwin wrote again about Peter Kürten in a book that dealt in the first part with some of the significant events in the evolution of criminology and finished with some thoughts on prevention and detection exposing his legal experience and opinions. The book was published by CA Watts & Co Ltd in 1956 and titled *Crime and Social Action.* In the middle of the nineteenth century the Italian Professor Cesare Lombroso formulated the view that the physical characteristics of the skull indicated criminal man. This turned attention from the study of crime to the study of the criminal. In Pavia and Turin he studied the skulls and other anatomical features of hundreds of prison inmates. He concluded that the criminal was revealed by his physical and mental anomalies as being apart from the race of normal mankind, differing from that race anatomically and psychologically, a creature foredoomed to a horrible destiny. Although his views were exaggerated and largely discarded he opened out a new field of exploration. Early in the twentieth century Dr Charles Goring, continuing on the work initiated by Dr Griffiths of the Prison Medical Service in Parkhurst Prison, made a statistical analysis of 3,000 prisoners. His findings indicated that there was no such thing as a physical criminal type. There is no criminal class, he concluded, but some individuals elected for the criminal way of life. In 1929, Professor Johannes Lange published his study of 35 pairs of twins in Bavaria. He saw some of the twins while they were serving sentences of imprisonment, some in his consulting room and others in their own homes. He concluded, that as far as crime is concerned, identical twins on the whole react in a definitely similar manner; non-identical twins behave quite differently. If, therefore, importance is attached to the Twins Method of investigation, it must be admitted that so far as the causes of crime are concerned innate tendencies play a preponderant part. At about the same time Professor Max Schlapp of the New York Post-graduate Medical School argued that the majority of criminals were the product of bodily disorders due to disturbances of the ductless glands and promoted the use of glandular extracts to treat criminal behaviour.

Later in the book Godwin reviewed many of the horrendous punishments that had been used throughout the ages for criminal behaviour, much of it in consequence of relatively minor harm. A gradual transition to less terrible punishment began with the treatise put forward by the Marchese di Beccaria in 1762. Godwin felt his theories of crimes and punishment had worn well. They might have been formulated in present times. In his book Godwin selected and condensed sections from that part of the treatise which had value and importance. He did not shy from his own view that capital punishment should be abolished to avoid those circumstances when it was later found to be wrongly administered.

At the end of the 1960s Godwin tried again to write a book because he felt he had to prove to himself that old age didn't necessarily mean complete feeble-mindedness. Sadly the book was never completed.

After publishing his last two books Godwin bought some neglected woodland that had been savaged by a contractor. He restored three acres and planted about two thousand three year old Norway fir transplants. When he toed in the last one he did so with a great sense of having achieved something worthwhile. Some years later he had to sell the plantation, which he hated doing, and the last time he saw it in semi-ruin an electric pylon was plain for all to see.

As mentioned earlier Godwin had written a book about the Surfleet Experiment and his interest in the land and the soil continued. In the war he and Dorothy grew vegetables in their garden in Cambridge and later he was able to buy at most reasonable price two old cottages on a narrow lane at Staplecross near Robertsbridge in Sussex. A modern end piece had been added by some previous owner. Again they tried to grow all vegetables that they required. Across the lane were seven acres of lovely woodland included with the house. In this they were really very fortunate for there was an established orchard that bore heavily and he unearthed a small vine. He bought a little greenhouse and set the vine under glass. It responded to this marvelously and yielded abundant crops of Hamburg grapes. Lying near the woods was a fine oak log. George had it lifted and taken to a sawmill and converted then left to dry out. From it he made a table from which he did his writing. The oak table had a top of two pieces two inches thick and dovetailed together. It was impressive for so guests exclaimed when they saw the well polished table. He built himself a good workshop in the garden and there, with a kit of tools he amused himself and built an oak chest and decorated it with thumb-wood carved to a home-made design. It looked rather nice. From an apple tree he fashioned a bellows for the fire. Monica now lived nearby at St Leonards near Hastings. It was only ten miles away and they could visit easily.

In his last years George lived very quietly, finding great pleasure in the garden, and in a renewed short correspondence with the occupational therapist that he had fallen in love with so many years ago in the Balfour Sanatorium in British Columbia.

# George Godwin Bibliography

*Columbia or the Future of Canada* (Kegan, 1928)

*Cain or the Future of Crime* (Kegan, 1928)

*The Eternal Forest Under Western Skies* (Appleton, 1929, Republished 1994, as "The Eternal Forest", by Godwin Books)

*Vancouver, a Life, 1757-98* (Allan, 1930)

*Why Stay We Here?* (Allan, 1930)

*Empty Victory* (Long, 1932)

*Discovery (The Story of the Finding of the World)* (Heath Cranton, 1933)

*The Disciple* (Acorn, 1936)

*Peter Kurten, A Study in Sadism* (Acorn, 1938)

*The Land Our Larder (the Suffleet Experiment)* (Acorn, 1939)

*Priest or Physician? A Study of Faith-healing* (Watts, 1941)

*Japan's New Order* (Watts, 1942)

*Queen Mary College* (1944)

*The Great Mystics* (Watts, 1945)

*Marconi (1939-45), a War Record* (Chatto and Windus, 1946)

*The Mystery of Anna Berger* (Watts, 1948)

*The Great Revivalists* (Watts, 1951)

*The Middle Temple* (Staples, 1954)

*Crime and Social Action* (London: Watts & co, 1956)

*Criminal Man* (NY Brazillar, 1957)